ESSIE MAE'S
DARK SECRETS

ESSIE MAE'S
DARK SECRETS

BETTY F. HAITH

LitPrime
"Your story is our priority"

LitPrime Solutions
21250 Hawthorne Blvd
Suite 500, Torrance, CA 90503
www.litprime.com
Phone: 1-800-981-9893

Published by LitPrime Solutions   03/20/2023

ISBN: 979-8-88703-160-6(sc)
ISBN: 979-8-88703-161-3(e)

Library of Congress Control Number: 2023902380

Contents

DEDICATION

This book is dedicated to my family.
For with God, all things are possible (Mark 10:27).

FOREWORD

Sometimes you can spend time with people, live with them, love them, and not really know what they've gone through, all because we didn't take the time to ask the right questions. An answer to a simple question can bring about revelations you never dreamed possible. People who have lived a long time have created lots of memories-some good and some not so good. The good memories are often shared without any prompting. But the bad ones may need to be lured out of the locked memory box of the soul, especially if they are as bad as Essie Mae's.

The story of Essie Mae Billings Bedford is fiction. However, there may be some who can relate to her story. Sometimes in our lives we make choices that we think are good, innocent, and full of fun at the time, not knowing the dangers and consequences that lurk in the shadows. Essie Mae's years of "having fun" left her with very few funny memories. Instead her memories seemed only to be of pain, remorse, and scars. If she had to compare her life of "having fun" to the life of living for the Lord, she would wholeheartedly advise you to skip the "having fun" part of life and go with living for the Lord. She would tell you it's safer, more peaceful, and the rewards are far greater.

Often people who have painful and ugly memories keep them buried to avoid facing or reliving an awful time in their lives or they'd rather keep them a secret to keep from embarrassing someone else. They may think even if the memories were made known, the unforgiveness and bitterness that has already taken root would not allow previously damaged relationships to be mended; so why bother? A good counselor might agree that those arguments may be valid, but not wise or healthy. It has been documented that confessing painful memories and freeing the conscious is a healthy thing to do because long-term bitterness and unforgiveness can cause serious health issues.

Essie Mae found sharing her horrible memories, however difficult it might have been, to be a burden lifting experience. After becoming a Bible-believing Christian in her golden years, she believed what she did was biblical after reading a passage found in James 5:16, "Therefore confess your sins to each other and pray for each other so that you may be healed." Essie Mae was compelled to confess her past before she died because she didn't want anything to prevent her from hearing that heavenly choir as she walked through those pearly gates!

CHAPTER 1

One very hot and muggy summer's day when every creature, great and small, sought air conditioning or shade of some sort to keep cool, there sat eighty-two-year- old Essie Mae and her sixteen year-old great-granddaughter on the porch fanning. Summer was in full force, with temperatures staying near ninety-five degrees for four days straight. With no air conditioning, there was just no place to find relief from the heat. Essie Mae and Nina sat on the porch, fanning out of habit only, because there was definitely no cool breeze coming from their efforts. They wore as little as possible-just enough to keep them decent. Nina wore short shorts and a halter, showing her youthful, shapely body, which reminded Essie Mae of herself in her younger days. Essie Mae wore a sleeveless cotton shift-dress covering her hefty hips and thighs. They drank a lot of ice water or lemonade while they sat on the porch and watched the few cars that went by. No one else was on their porches;

they were inside in the comfort of their air conditioning. When the weather wasn't so hot, the neighborhood was lively with children playing and neighbors chatting and teenagers gathering to play ball or talk about girlfriends or boyfriends. But it was just too hot for any of that on a day as hot as this day.

Essie Mae loved her neighborhood; everyone got along, went to church, and looked out for one another. There were no drug problems that she had heard of, and most of the children stayed in school until they graduated. She believed one of the reasons her neighborhood was so nice was because she prayed for it every night. And when she took her evening walk in the cool of the day, she'd pray for the different families as she passed their homes. She felt blessed to live there.

She loved sitting on her porch in the evening, when it was cool, and watching the children play or talking to her neighbors, especially Lula who lived across the street. Essie Mae knew If Lula had been home, Lula would have called over to see why she was sitting on the porch in near ninety- five-degree weather, and she would have invited her into her cool, comfortable home. But Lula was away visiting her daughter. Although it was hot and muggy, Essie Mae and Nina both felt they could make it until relief came.

"What a time for the air conditioner to go out," Essie Mae said for the umpteenth time.

"It's all right, Grandma, we only have five hours until your new unit arrives. Besides, it's not all that bad," Nina insisted.

"Maybe you should go home and come back when the new unit is in," Essie Mae said for another umpteenth time.

"No, Grandma, I'll wait with you," Nina replied as she had the times before.

To help take their mind off the heat, Nina brought up a subject that always made the time pass quickly-her great-grandma's childhood. She could listen to those stories for hours. Nina had enjoyed spending her summers with Grandma Essie since she was five years old. Now she was sixteen and wouldn't think of missing spending at least part of her summer at "Grandma's house." Her brothers used to accompany her, but they'd gotten involved with summer camp and softball, which took the place of "going to Grandma's." Even Nina knew eventually her summers would be full of summer jobs and other activities and even she would have to cut short her summer visits. But for now, she thought, I will enjoy this summer no matter how hot it is. Even though the air conditioner was broken, she was still in her most favorite place in the world and wouldn't trade it for anything.

All the many summers Nina had stayed at Grandma Essie's house, she had heard stories of how Grandma Essie grew up. She knew some of the stories from memory. But she still loved to hear Grandma Essie retell them. So she asked a question that kept Essie Mae busy until the truck came with the new air conditioner several hours later.

"Grandma, was it ever this hot when you were growing up on the farm?" Nina asked.

"Child, yeah," Essie Mae responded as she stopped fanning long enough to get a drink of ice water from the glass that sat near her chair. Nina knew she was in for some interesting stories.

"We had to work the fields in heat like this, chopping weeds from the corn field or the garden, or pulling worms off the tobacco so they wouldn't eat the plants.

"How did you get the worms off?" Nina asked

"We pulled them off with our hands, silly. How else were we going to get them off? We'd walk from plant to plant, lifting each leaf looking for worms. If we found one, we'd pull it off, throw it to the ground, and stomp it with our foot. The big, fat green ones, the boys could throw them so hard to the ground that they would splash open."

"Ugh," Nina said, making a face. "I could never do that deliberately pick up a worm. Ugh," she said again with a shudder.

"We didn't like it either, but we had to do it. We'd come in for dinner (the noon meal was called dinner back in those days) around noon, and after we ate, we'd rest under the shade trees for about an hour or so and then back to the field. It was never too hot to work in the fields."

"What do you mean by shade trees, Grandma?" Nina asked.

"The shade trees were our air conditioning. We had about five or six maple trees clustered together near the house that we referred to as the shade trees. That's where we gathered for all kinds of events during the summer, like family reunions, entertaining company, or we'd even take a nap on a palate, which is a quilt or a blanket on the ground, if the flies weren't too bad. The flies were some pesky little things. They'd alight on your face, in your food- everywhere. I hated those buggas!" Essie Mae laughed. "They were everywhere, in the kitchen when you were trying to cook or eat, in the bedroom when you're trying to sleep, or if you were just trying to carry on a conversation, they were there pestering you. The only time you got a break from them was during the winter months. It was too cold for them then. But as soon as spring and summer came, they were back. No matter how many we killed by spraying, setting out fly bait, or using a fly swatter, you could never get rid of them. The more you killed, the more returned, it seemed. Thank God they are not as bad now as they were then. They were almost like the plague in the Bible when God sent flies because Pharaoh wouldn't let the Israelites go. You remember that story, don't you, Child?"

As far back as Nina could remember, Grandma Essie lovingly called her "Child." When she was four or five, she fell and skinned her knee. Blood was running down her leg, and it hurt something terrible. Mama was trying to clean it, but Nina remembered how she was screaming to the top of her lungs. Then Grandma Essie appeared and said, "Bring the child to me." Grandma Essie picked her up and placed her on her lap and wrapped her loving arms around her and with a soothing voice said, "There, there, Child, it's going to be all right." Suddenly the pain was not so great and the blood was not so scary. Nina believed that was the moment when her heart became knitted to her Grandma Essie's heart.

"Yes, Grandma, I remember the story about the flies. It's in Exodus, chapter eight," Nina said with confidence.

"I'm proud of you," Essie Mae said. "I see you have been paying attention in Sunday school. Sister Madge must be a good teacher."

"We all love Sister Madge. She makes learning about the Bible interesting. She always encourages us to learn chapter and verse so we can quote it when we refer to the Bible," Nina said.

"That's good. You keep on learning, Child," Essie Mae insisted.

"Yes, Ma'am. So, when did you stop working in the fields?" Nina asked, leading her Grandma back to the subject.

"When I turned sixteen and could date. I found me a boy who wanted to marry me, and I said yes just to get away from that hard work. Then I found out I had to work hard a different way. Having babies is hard work, Child, and don't you forget it. The pain of having them and then you're up all night with them crying. So don't you have any babies until you are married, because your old grandma's too old to help you take care of a baby. You hear me, Child?

"Yes, Grandma," Nina said.

"Don't you be like some of these fast-tail gals out

here getting pregnant before they know what having a baby is all about. Babies having babies. Don't you let no little fast boy talk you into giving your all to him, you hear me?"

"Yes, Grandma," Nina said, remembering the two girls in her school who were walking around with big stomachs just before school let out. She didn't want to go through that embarrassment.

Essie Mae had gotten off the subject again, and Nina wanted to hear more.

Each time Essie Mae told the story, Nina would hear something new. She thought of writing a book about it all one day-maybe after college. She knew she had writing abilities. Her English teacher had taken a liking to her short stories and essays for school and had begun to encourage her to pursue a career in writing. She'd say, "Nina, you have a way with words. I enjoy reading your work. You have great potential for writing. Promise me you won't let that talent go to waste." Nina promised she wouldn't because she loved to write and she felt a promise like that would be easy to keep.

As she sat fanning, she looked a Grandma Essie, who turned eighty-two that year. She complained of arthritis in her shoulders and fingers, but other than that, she was healthy and her mind was sharp. Nina looked at the ugly scars on Grandma Essie's arms, shoulders, and neck. She could see them well today because she was wearing a sleeveless dress. Essie Mae normally wore sleeves to cover the scars. Nina wondered if she should ask how she got them. She never really heard the whole story. Her mama and aunts rarely mentioned Grandma Essie's scars. If they did, they referred to them as "her accident." But they would never go into details. It was as if they were afraid to talk about it. Nina had been curious about it for a long time but hesitated to ask anybody. Suddenly she felt the urge to ask. She didn't want to hurt or embarrass her great-grandma, but she felt this would be a good time to ask while she was in a nostalgic mood as they waited for the delivery of the air conditioner.

"Grandma Essie, may I ask you something?"

"Sure, Child, what is it?"

"How'd you get those scars? "Immediately, Essie Mae reached up and rubbed a hand over the scars. Memories flooded her mind. Then she said, "Child, go get your old grandma a big glass of water and I'll tell you all about it. I've kept those dark memories buried for years. I guess no one has ever had the nerve to ask me about them, except you. And I have had a need to share it with someone here lately to free my soul. I don't want nothing standing in my way when I meet my Maker. Now go on and get that water. Make sure you put some ice in it!" she yelled at Nina as she ran into the house, letting the screen door slam.

"Okay, Grandma," Nina called back and rushed to get the ice water. She was anxious to hear a story she hadn't heard before but had wondered about for years.

CHAPTER 2

Essie Mae took a long drink of the cool ice water, picked up the rhythm of her rocking and fanning, and drifted back into time to begin to tell her story. Before she did, she said to Nina, "I hope your little innocent ears will be able to handle what I'm about to tell you."

That made Nina that much more excited! "Oh, Grandma, I'm not a baby, I've heard a lot of stuff, " Nina said, trying to sound more grown up than her young sixteen years.

"But nothing like what you're about to hear, my Child," Essie Mae assured her.

"It can't be that bad, Grandma. I can handle it," Nina said, more intrigued than ever.

"Okay. May the Good Lord protect your young spirit," Essie Mae said as she gave in to Nina's insistence.

"Well, let's see," Essie Mae began. "I got married when I wasn't much older than you. I met this nice boy

9

named Jocko Waller at church one Sunday. We started courting after he got up enough nerve to ask Daddy's permission. We started courting when I was sixteen and got married a year later so I wouldn't have to work in the fields, remember?" Essie Mae smiled at Nina.

"You mean, the boy had to ask your daddy if he could date you?" Nina said in surprise.

"Yeah, Child. Back then we had to show respect to all of our elders. Anyway, after we courted for about a year, he popped the question. I immediately said yes because I thought getting married would save me from all the hard work Mama and Daddy was putting on me. We were married, and we were happy. When we were able to get a small place of our own, I was very happy. I didn't like staying with his family. When we got our place, we started having babies. We had a boy first. This made Jocko so happy. Then I had three girls-Gail, Barbara, and Sharon. Gail was your grandma." Nina knew her grandma's name was Gail, but she never knew her; she died when she was a baby.

"I used to dress my children up on Sunday and we'd all go to church," Essie Mae continued. "That was one thing Mama and Daddy taught us children-go to church on Sunday. Mama and Daddy also tried to teach us to be good Christian children-no smoking, drinking, cussing, and running around with all kinds of different men and women. Those who did those things were sinners . But to me, it looked like those who were doing all those things were the ones having all the fun. I wanted to have fun just like them. I started having fun when I married Jocko. Jocko loved his whisky. At first I didn't drink because it burned my insides, plus Mama and Daddy said it was wrong. But I wanted to share things with Jocko, so I learned to tolerate it. It made me feel giddy and lightheaded, and it made me laugh a lot. All the guilty feelings I used to get from being a sinner slowly faded away. Every Saturday night was our drinking night, but every Sunday I went to church and asked the Lord to forgive me for sinning . Then one day, tragedy struck. My Jocko was dead-dropped dead of a heart attack. That was something we never thought about because we were so young. Only old people died, I thought. What was I going to do without Jocko? How was I going to take care of four children? The little money I made cleaning house for a rich white lady didn't go that far. With the help of the welfare department, I found this small, cheap apartment, and we moved in. I was so embarrassed to have to rely on the government for help. With all the children Mama and Daddy had, they never had to depend on the government for help. They worked hard and depended on the Lord to bless them through other people who would give them used clothes, meat when they killed hogs, or vegetables or fruits if they had abundance. People on welfare were looked upon as *po folk.'* But I couldn't do any better, and I had to swallow my pride for the children's sake. The five of us soon adjusted to that small four-room apartment-kitchen, living room, and two bedrooms. I continued to clean house for the white lady. She'd give me leftover food, and I'd take it home to the children.

This helped out a lot. Sometimes on Sundays we'd get a ride to go see Mama and Daddy and if the garden was in, we'd get vegetables to take home. The children loved to visit their grandma and grandpa. My children were about the same age as some of my younger sisters and brothers. Mama was still having children when my sister and I were old enough to become mothers. She gave birth to fourteen children. The Sundays we visited Mama she'd have a big Sunday dinner cooked and we'd all gather around the long table and eat until we were full. Mama sure was a good cook."

"You're a good cook too, Grandma!" Nina interrupted." I love your biscuits, and your banana pudding is to die for!

"I learned from your great-great grandma. She could stretch a little food to make it so a crowd would get enough. It was like Jesus when he fed the multitude with two fish and five loaves of bread. What Scripture is that found in, Child?" Essie Mae asked Nina.

"Mark 6," Nina said confidently.

Essie Mae looked at her and smiled and continued her story.

"But when it came to me feeding my four children, food didn't go very far. I was always trying to stretch a dollar by buying cheap stuff like peanut butter and crackers. Then the Lord blessed me to get a job in a cafe as a cook. I made a little more money, and I got to take home leftovers every night. Hamburgers and hotdogs became a regular meal in our house.

"It was at that cafe that men started to show interest

in me," Essie Mae continued. "I noticed if I acted real friendly, they left me a tip. So I started smiling more. One day Valjean, the girl I worked with at the cafe, invited me to go to a party with her. I hadn't gone anywhere but to church and to town since Jocko died. Two years had passed. I was too busy raising my children. Valjean continued to urge me, and I relented after several weeks of her begging me. My children then were ages thirteen, eleven, ten, and eight. I asked a neighbor to listen out for them. The children knew how to behave and to stay in the house when I wasn't there. But I never left them alone at night, and I was nervous about it. So I thought I'd better leave someone for them to go to in case of an emergency. I tried to back out several times, but Valjean wouldn't hear of it. I believed her when she told me I was still young and I needed a life other than my children. I was in my early thirties, and I had a nice shape, a beautiful smile, and a contagious laugh, someone said. I used to see men looking at me, but I paid them no mind. I was not interested. I still loved Jocko."

"Did you go to the party, Grandma?" Nina asked.

"Yeah, honey. I went, and that was the beginning of my downfall. The quiet, demure, churchgoing Essie Mae got lost that night," Essie Mae said in a tone full of remorse.

"What do you mean, Grandma? What happened?" Nina was anxious to hear.

"My dear Child, let me tell you. You are not going

to be proud of your great-grandmother when you hear the rest of my story," Essie Mae said.

"That was in the past, Grandma. You're saved now, right?" Nina said, insinuating that once you're saved all your past is forgiven.

"You're right, Child," Essie Mae agreed and continued her story.

"The party was at somebody's house I didn't know, but Valjean did. At the door, I was so nervous that Valjean held my hand real tight and said, 'Come on. You'll have fun.' The door opened and there were guys standing around with cigarettes and whisky glasses in their hands. Some of the girls smoked, too. The smoke almost stifled me. Valjean, still holding my hand, worked her way over to someone she knew and introduced me. She handed me a drink, and I took it. Then a guy walked over to Valjean and said, 'Who's your friend?' She introduced me. The rest of the night he tried to talk to me. I didn't mind too much; it gave me something to do since I didn't know anyone there but Valjean. The music started playing. I hadn't danced in a long time. Jim, that was the guy's name, asked me to dance. No one else was on the floor. I reluctantly said yes. When I started moving to the rhythm of the music, something inside me started to wake up. I started having fun and really getting into the dance steps. Suddenly we had an audience. Any other time I would have been embarrassed to have a group of people watch me dance. But the more they watched, the more I enjoyed it, and I really put on a show for them with my body moving to the beat of the music. After the music stopped, we went outside to cool off. Jim said, 'I like the way you dance, Essie Mae, and I just love the way you laugh. How about going out with me next week? I'll take you dancing.' I said yes, and that was the beginning of all my troubles.

"Why, Grandma? It was just a date. Did you have fun? Wasn't he nice to you?" Nina asked.

"Oh, he was very nice. Actually, he was a perfect gentleman. I dated him a while, and occasionally I went to parties with Valjean. At those parties I met guys that smoked and drank and cussed-rough men. Somehow or other they appealed to me more so than Jim, who was nice and kind. Jim took an interest in my children and bought them gifts. The children loved him. He even mentioned getting married and helping me take care of them. It should have been what I wanted, but I put him off.

"One night while out with Valjean, I met this rough, foul mouth man who took a liking to me. In turn, I liked him too. No decent woman would give him the time of day. But when he called my name, I was right there. I started avoiding Jim until he got the message and stopped coming around.

"Don't you ever do that, Nina. You hear me? You look for a nice Christian man to marry. You hear me, Child?" Essie Mae couldn't stress that enough to Nina. She didn't want her to suffer even a fraction of the pain she had suffered.

"Yes, Grandma. I promise," Nina said, confused at the serious look on Essie Mae's face.

"Anyway," Essie Mae began again, "by me being so infatuated with him-Lloyd was his name. I gave him anything he wanted and when he wanted it. Before long I found out that I was pregnant. I told Lloyd, and he told me to get rid of it. He knew a woman that would help me. But I couldn't do that. Even though I'd stopped going to church, Mama's teachings were instilled in me. When he found out that I wasn't going to get rid of it, he hit me hard in the stomach, trying to make me lose it. I hurt for days. But the pain soon subsided and I continued on with the pregnancy. After that he found another woman and never looked my way again. I was so hurt. And guess who helped me out during that time? Jim. He was so nice to me. I had another boy. I named him Benjamin. As soon as I saw him, I could tell something was wrong with him. He was mentally retarded. I kept him for a while and then I put him in a school so he could be helped. I always believed it happened because Lloyd punched me in the stomach."

"What happened to him, Grandma? I have never heard anyone speak of him," Nina inquired.

"I used to go visit him as often as I could. But as time went by, I stopped going. The school would write and let me know his progress. When he was about twenty-five years old, I got a letter from the school saying he could be released to come home, but I had no room for him. I didn't feel I could care for a mentally retarded man no more than I could have tended to a mentally retarded baby. So I ignore the letter. About ten years later, a letter came to inform me that Benjamin had died in his sleep one night. I felt sad and guilty. I had abandoned him, and he never knew his mother's love. I have cried to the Lord many times asking for forgiveness for my selfish act toward Benjamin."

"I'm sure the Lord has forgiven you, Grandma. You're such a loving person," Nina said with compassion. "Do you want some lemonade?"

"I'll get it. I have to go to the little girls' room anyway," Essie Mae said. "I'll be back to continue the story. There is so much more to tell."

In a few minutes, Essie Mae came back onto the porch with a glass of lemonade. Nina hadn't moved. She was anxious to hear the rest of the story. She could hardly believe what she had heard so far. Not Grandma Essie! Essie Mae took a sip of the delicious lemonade and continued her story-fanning as she spoke using a folded newspaper.

"A while after Benjamin was born, I met another rough guy," Essie Mae continued. "He loved to party and drink beer. He didn't mind buying mine either. We ran around together for a year or so until he got tired of me and found someone new-fresh meat,' as they used to say. I was disappointed for a while, but before long I had hooked up with someone else. I was never alone for long. I was getting a reputation as a 'good-time gal.' Before long I was pregnant again. This time I had a girl-your great aunt Gilda. Then in a couple of years came your great uncle Percy. In a few more years, along came your great aunt Sarah. All had different daddies, and none of the daddies took an interest in his child."

Nina could hardly believe what she was hearing. No way could her great-grandmother be the person she was describing.

"Listen, Child, I know you are shocked at what I'm telling you. But it's all true. I'm ashamed to admit it, but it's all true," Essie Mae said looking at Nina, seeming to read her thoughts. "I have lived a rough life and after I changed; after God cleaned me up, I never wanted to talk about those old times. I wanted to keep them buried deep within me. For some reason I have this need to share this with somebody so my conscience can be clear. All of this is leading up to the answer to your question of how I got these scars. Do you want to hear the rest of my life story? Just say the word and I will stop right here. But if you feel you can handle it, I'll continue."

"Oh, Grandma, I'm shocked that you have gone through all this. I never would have believed it knowing who you are now. But since you are the one to tell me, I have to believe it. I've been thinking that I would write a book about you, Grandma, but I thought it would be on the many nice things you have done for others, how good a cook you are, and things like that. But this is more than I ever dreamed of."

Essie Mae looked into Nina's eyes and said, "You can write all about this, Child. Feel free to tell everything I tell you as long as you tell how Jesus came into my life and cleansed me and saved me and made me into a new woman."

"Grandma, do you mind if I use my tape recorder so I won't miss anything?"

"Run on in the house and get it, Child. I'll wait for you."

In a matter of minutes, Nina was back with her tape recorder ready for the rest of Grandma Essie's incredible life story.

CHAPTER 3

"After Sarah was born, I stopped having babies, but rarely visited Mama and Daddy during that time. I was too embarrassed. I was living contrary to the way I was brought up. My other sisters and brothers were living clean lives, married, and working hard to make a home for their families. I felt like the 'black sheep' of the family with all my illegitimate children. When I did visit Mama, she would beg me to straighten up and start going back to church before something bad happened to me. She had heard what kind of men I ran around with. I would promise I would, but as soon as I left her, I continued to have my fun. So to keep from hearing her beg me, I just stayed away from her.

"By now Jocko Jr. was old enough to start going out. Before I knew it, he was acting like the guys I was hanging out with. He started drinking, and he couldn't hold a job. He would lie around the house and sleep off a drunk most of the week. I tried to talk him into getting a job. I heard myself sounding like Mama-begging him to change his life. But he just wanted to run the streets and get drunk and come home and sleep it off. He'd stagger down the street, and cars would swerve to keep from hitting him. I'd beg him to be careful and not to walk home when he was drunk. I was so afraid he would get hit by a car. And that's exactly what happened. I was at work when his sister called me and told me that Junior had been hit by a car and that he was dead. I'll always remember that awful stabbing pain I felt inside when she said, 'He's dead.' I knew there would not be another chance to try to get him to change. I felt if I had been a better mother, he would not have turned out the way he did. I mourned for about a month. I didn't feel like partying or drinking. I lay around the house remembering how happy Jocko was when I presented him with his son, how he always planned for things to be so much better for Junior than they were for him. All those plans died when he died and poor Junior was left with no one to encourage him or to guide him. I was too busy 'having fun.'"

"Shortly after that Gail started dating and fell in love. Before I knew it she was pregnant and talking about marriage. She found her a good man with a good family that went to church a lot . His family loved Gail, and she loved them. Sometimes I thought she wished his mother was her mother. Gail acted like she was ashamed of me sometimes. I know I embarrassed her with my drinking and sleeping around with so many different men. She avoided me like I avoided my own mother. I knew how Mama felt. Still I was glad she had a good husband and a good home. You are a lot like your grandmother, you know," she said, looking at Nina.

"Yeah. Mama says that a lot. I wish she hadn't died so soon so I could have spent more time with her," Nina said. "But I'm glad I have you, Grandma Essie," Nina said, smiling.

"I'm glad you have me too." Essie Mae smiled back and continued her story.

"Now Barbara was different. She took after me. She was wild and loved to drink, dance, and cuss. She loved men and had her share of them. Sometimes we even double dated and went to clubs together. Barbara began having babies by different men, too. She was following right in her mother's footsteps. She found a girlfriend who was just as wild as she, and the two often got into trouble. I, more than once, had to go to the police station to bail her out. She got arrested for such things as disorderly conduct in public, destruction of property, and even shoplifting. Because she had been arrested several times before, when she got arrested for shoplifting, she was sent to jail. She was in jail for about six months.

"By the time she got out of jail, me and Valjean had moved to another city at the encouragement of, as you might guess, a man. We found us a housekeeping job and a two-bedroom apartment and started our new lives. "There were so many clubs in that city. So many men we hadn't met. Nobody knew us, so we attracted the eyes of many men. Of course I wound up with the worst of them all.

"In the meantime, my three illegitimate children grew up. They practically raised themselves. I didn't have time for children. Their outcome proved that. Gilda moved upstate when she was about seventeen. No one knew exactly what or how she was doing up there. She ran off with some no-good boy. After about two years, we got a call to say that Gilda had been found dead. The police thought her death had something to do with prostitution. We never knew for sure. Barbara and a friend went to claim the body and brought her home for burial. We mourned for a week and then went back to having fun. Percy started hanging around with some boys up to no good. A few years after we buried Gilda, Percy was dead. They said someone pushed him in front of an oncoming car – a prank that went too far. All of my illegitimate children were dead except Sarah. She probably would have followed them if I hadn't given her away to her father's family. His mother always wanted a little girl, and I knew I couldn't take care of another baby. When she asked for her, I was delighted to let her go. That decision probably saved her life. She was raised in a loving home. She graduated and went to a business school and got a good job. I was so proud of her."

CHAPTER 4

"It was after I moved to the city that I found out how bad things could really get. Maybe if I had stayed home, in familiar territory, I would not have suffered so much. You asked me how I got these scars. This little carefree, fun-loving, country girl went to the city, thinking she could handle any man with a little sweet talk and sexual pleasures, like she did at home. But she soon found out differently."

Nina was concentrating hard, getting ready to hear what bad things happened to cause such awful scars on Grandma Essie's body. Suddenly, Grandma broke her concentration by asking, "Isn't that the icecream man coming? It sounds like the music."

Nina had blocked out the heat and everything else while listening to Grandma Essie's interesting story and she hadn't heard the ice cream truck with its catchy tune. The street, which had been empty all the time they had been sitting on the porch, was suddenly filled with children coming from every house.

"Run out there and get us a snow cone, Child. That would certainly cool us off."

"Ah, Grandma, couldn't you just continue the story? I don't want a snow cone right now."

"Well, I do. Now go on in there and get the money off the dresser and get us a snow cone. Bring me a grape one."

Nina saw that she wasn't about to change her mind, so she ran quickly to get the money and ran to the ice cream truck and joined the crowd. She saw a couple of girlfriends among the crowd.

"Hey, Nina, want to come over and listen to some records?" they asked.

Any other time Nina would have jumped at the invitation. But today, she had other things on her mind.

"No. I can't today. My Grandma is without air conditioning, and I'm keeping her company while she waits for the new one to come this afternoon. Maybe another time, okay?"

She got her two snow cones and hurried back to her grandmother's porch. Essie Mae loved snow cones. She was careful not to eat it too fast lest she got a headache. She hated those headaches when she ate those things too fast. Nina wanted her to eat and talk, but she didn't ask her. She tried to sit back and enjoy her snow cone as much as Essie Mae seemed to enjoy hers. The crushed ice did cool them off for a spell.

"Now, where was I?" Essie Mae asked after she had

leisurely eaten her grape snow cone-remarking several times how good it was, and when she had finished, went inside to wash her hands. Now that she was back in her rocking chair, she was ready to resume her story–to Nina's great delight! She quickly quoted the last sentences Essie Mae had said to bring her back on track:

"You and Valjean had moved to the city, found jobs and an apartment. You went there with the same attitude you had back home and thought your way of handling men with sweet talk and sexual pleasures would get you the same results there, but they didn't," Nina summarized.

"Wow! Is that what I said?" Grandma said, teasing.

"Ah, Grandma," Nina said, smiling. "What happened next?"

"When Barbara got out of jail, she came and lived with Valjean and me for a while. Then her girlfriend moved there, and they got an apartment together not far from us. Sometimes we'd go to the clubs together, and other times they did their own thing. But we were close and kept in touch with one another every day. Barbara was still wild and crazy. Jail had not tamed her. Sometimes she was even too wild for me, so we didn't go clubbing together very often. But she was with me and Valjean when I met Jake. Who would have known I would regret it the rest of my life? I still remember the night we met."

Suddenly, Essie Mae changed the subject and said, "Nina, baby, do you think we could get a bite to eat before I finish my story? I'm getting a little hungry. Why don't you go and make us a couple of sandwiches?"

What prompted her to stop at that moment, she wasn't sure. Maybe she dreaded dredging up that awful period in her life, or maybe she was truly hungry and needed strength to finish her story. She knew she didn't have to tell the whole horrible story, but somehow she seemed compelled to open the door and let the terrible dark secrets out anyway.

Nina didn't argue this time. They had been talking a very long time and she was hungry too. She rushed into the kitchen, leaving Essie Mae to her thoughts. In about thirty minutes Nina was back carrying a tray with sandwiches of sliced ham with lettuce and tomato and mayonnaise, chips, and some of the oatmeal cookies they had baked the day before, and two large glasses of lemonade with ice. The ice tinkled against the glass as she walked. As they settled back to munch on their sandwiches, a gentle breeze cooled them.

"Umm, this is a good sandwich, Nina. I didn't realize how hungry I was," Essie said. "You know, while you were in the kitchen, I was thinking how on a day like this Mama would make homemade ice cream. Those were special times. The ice cream would be so good, creamy, and cold. We should make some."

"How did you make homemade ice cream?"

"We had this wooden bucket with a small hole in the side for water to run out and a crank that attached to the top. Mama mixed milk, sugar, and flavoring and put it in the container that sat in the center of the bucket. We'd pack crushed ice and rock salt around it and cranked it until it got hard to crank. We'd all take turns cranking. Oh, the anticipation! When it got too hard to crank, we knew the milk had turned to ice cream. It tasted so sweet, creamy, and cold. We would try to eat our first serving fast so we could get seconds. If we ate it too fast, we'd get an awful headache."

"A brain freeze, we call it," Nina said.

"When we were kids, making homemade ice cream was as exciting as Christmas. Before you leave this summer, we'll make some. We'll have to go shopping to get what we need."

"That sounds like fun, Grandma. Now that we've finished eating, are you ready to finish telling your story?" She couldn't wait to see what happened next.

"Of course, Child," Essie Mae said. She was surprised that Nina was so interested. She didn't think anyone could be interested in her awful life.

Before Nina could push the button of her tape recorder, Essie Mae said, "Do you know what else would taste good? A nice cold watermelon. We used to grow them, you know. We would pick one from the field and place it in a cold tub of water to cool it off. Watermelons then were sweet. It's hard to find a real sweet one in the grocery stores these days."

"Grandma, are you stalling?" Nina asked. "If you don't want to finish telling the story, I'll understand. As much as I want to hear it, I don't want you to tell me if the memories are too painful."

"I guess I am stalling a little. I haven't brought those

memories to mind in fifty years. Most of the people that knew me then are dead. But I want people to know what God can do. I want them to know that the love of Jesus can change anyone. There is nothing too hard for him. He forgives and can make you a new person, just like being reborn. That's what he's done for me. The person that I'll describe to you Nina, honey, will not be me. You will not believe that it was ever me. But when you push Jesus out of your life and start living for the devil, his influence can make you do awful things. He will make you think you are having fun, but in the end he will try to kill you. The Bible says the devil has come to kill, steal, and destroy.

"John 10:10," Nina piped in voluntarily. Essie Mae smiled, but continued. "When people give the devil control of their lives, he does just that-kill, steal, and destroy it. Baby, don't you ever live for the devil. Always keep Christ in your life. Do you hear me, Child?"

"Yes, Grandma," Nina said, feeling kind of sad. She felt her question had caused her grandmother to relive some painful memories. She kind of wished she hadn't asked. But she was still intrigued as to what were the awful secret memories she had kept buried within for fifty years. Now that she had knocked on the sealed door of those memories and Essie Mae had promised to open it for her, should she let her do it? Would it be too painful for her? Would those old memories haunt her after she finally spoken them out loud? "Dear Jesus," she prayed, "if this is wrong, give me the strength to tell my grandmother that I really don't want to hear her secrets. Then she could keep them buried forever. I really don't need to know. I am just curious about the scars. I may be learning more than how she got the scars-more than what I need or want to know. Please stop her from telling me if it's going to cause her pain. Please, Jesus!" she prayed.

"I think I'm ready now. Where did I stop?" Essie Mae said, interrupting Nina's prayer. "Grandma, you don't have to tell me anymore if you don't want to. I didn't realize ..."

"It's all right, Baby. I'm not afraid of the memories. For a moment I was embarrassed for Jesus' sake. But you know what? He has forgiven me for all my sins, and he doesn't remember them anymore. I have the Holy Ghost in me. He will protect me from any lingering memories after I've shared the rest of the story. So you see, I'm okay. Don't feel bad for me," Essie Mae said, reaching over and taking Nina's hand to reassure her. It is sweet of you to be concerned about your old great-grandma. Now where did I stop?"

Just then a truck pulled into the driveway.

"Look, Grandma, the air conditioning man is here!" Nina said.

"Is it 5:00 already? We've been talking so much that the time just flew by. Come on in here," Essie Mae call out to the man. "What took you so long? I've been burning up all day!" she said playfully.

"I got here as soon as I could, Ma'am. It's been a terribly hot day and everyone's been suffering. I'll have you cool in no time," he reassured her.

"Come on, Nina, let's see what we can get from the garden."

The rest of the story had automatically been put on hold. They strolled to the backyard to check for some ripe tomatoes, cucumbers, squash, onions, and hopefully some okra. While they were checking the vines, Nina asked, "Grandma why do you plant a garden each year when you can buy the same vegetables in the grocery store? It would be less work on you."

"I don't mind the work. I love it. I plant a garden because I love to work the soil, plant the seeds, and watch them grow. I guess the farm life has never really left me. Evenings like this we, my sisters and brothers, would follow Mama to the garden to gather food to cook for our meals. Gathering vegetables from my own garden keeps me young at heart. And when I taste a ripe, juicy tomato, I'm a child again! They are so good. The vegetables you get from the store are not half this good. This is straight from God's good earth. It hasn't been doctored up like that stuff you get from the grocery store. Oh, look, the okra is ready to be picked. We'll have some for supper!"

About that time the man yelled to them that the unit was in and working fine. They would be cool and comfortable in a few minutes. They thanked him, and he was on his way.

It was good to be in a cool house again. They cooked their vegetables, ate dinner, and washed the dishes-chatting about insignificant things. Later they each took a shower and retreated to their separate bedrooms.

Nina lay in bed and thought about all she had heard about her precious grandmother. Essie Mae lay in her bed thinking about what was left to tell. She read her Bible and talked to the Lord about her feelings and her decision to share her past with Nina. By the time she had finished praying, she had peace in her heart about finally telling all of her deep dark secrets. She didn't know if Nina would tell anyone right away, or if she would wait until she was older to write her book. By then, there would probably be no one left who could remember the story to verify its validity. Everyone would probably think it was Nina's vivid imagination-which was something she truly had. No matter how the story would be received, Essie Mae didn't really care. After all, that was the old Essie Mae. She was a brand new person and loved who she was.

Before dawn they were awakened by some sharp lightning and some deep rolls of thunder and then the heavy downpour. After such a hot day before, an electrical storm was no surprise. They both lingered in bed a little longer than usual since it was raining. But before too long, Nina heard Essie Mae stirring about. But she dozed back off to sleep. It wasn't too long before she was awakened by the aroma of hot biscuits. When she entered the kitchen, Essie Mae said, "I knew the smell of my biscuits would get you out of that bed."

"Do you think it's going to rain all day, Grandma?" Nina asked.

"I expect so," she answered.

"What are we going to do? Television is boring during the day."

"I thought I would finish telling my story if you are still interested."

"Yes, I'm still interested," she said with gladness. "But I kinda thought you didn't want to talk about it anymore."

"I considered not going any further with it, but I think the Lord is pleased with my decision to go on. I feel at peace anyway. Let's go into the sunroom. This is where I love to sit and meditate and commune with the Lord. This is my favorite place in the house. Let's sit out here. It's so cozy, don't you agree?"

"Yes, I love it out here too."

"Do you have your tape recorder ready? Now where did I stop? I'm sure you remember."

"I remember. You were about to meet Jake. The day you will regret for the rest of your life," Nina said without hesitation.

"Oh, yeah. I remember that Saturday night. Me and Valjean had on our tight skirts and blouses. We had fixed our hair and put on makeup. We were on the prowl. Barbara and her girlfriend came along that night. The four of us were men hungry. We chose a club we'd heard about where a lot of men hung out. When we got there the jukebox was jumping, smoke filled the air, and there were a lot of men-hungry women already there. There were a few men there, and more kept coming and going. We got us a table where we could see everyone. We sized up the men and commented on the ones who were handsome or ugly, too short or too fat. After a while we saw girls rushing up to this one guy as he walked in and they seemed to sing-Hello, J-a-k-e!' When I saw him I could see why. I wanted to sing his name too. Here walks in this tall, lanky, dark-skinned guy, with slicked back hair, shiny white teeth, and a dip in his walk. 'Lardy mercy, look at him. He's mine!' I told the girls. But Valjean said, 'With all those girls hanging on him, you don't stand a chance.' I told her, 'Watch and see. That man will be mine before the night is over.'

"Like I told you before, my attitude was if I wanted it, I'd find a way to get it-and I wanted J-a-k-e," Essie Mae said, mimicking those girls back then. Essie Mae and Nina chuckled. Then Essie Mae continued. "After he had shaken all the girls off his arms, he strolled over to the bar and stood looking at the crowd. He knew he had charm, and he knew all the women wanted him. While he stood at the bar, I pretended I was going to speak with a friend across the room. I got up and walked in front of him and oh so slowly paused and looked into his eyes and smiled ever so slightly and walked away. I could feel his eyes on me; therefore, I swayed my hips dramatically. I only stayed a minute or two and headed back to my table. On the way back, I did a repeat and swayed my hips more and sat down. Just then a song came on the jukebox that I loved to dance to. Before long Jake was extending his hand across the table saying, 'May I have this dance?' His voice went right along with the rest of his good looks. I said, 'Of course,' in my most feminine voice. As I strutted to the dance floor with my hand in Jake's, I looked back at my friends and gave them a look that said, 'See. I told you so.' They just laughed and said, 'Essie Mae, you're good!'

"He could dance too. You know I couldn't let him outdo me. I was doing moves that I didn't know I could do. We had just about everybody's attention. The more people watched, the more we put into it. When that song was over, a slow song began to play. He pulled me to him, and we started dancing slow. I didn't resist at all. I pressed my body against him, and our bodies were swaying this way and that way to the music. When the music stopped, he suggested that we go outside to cool off. He led me out side. As we were going out the door, I heard one of the girls who were hanging on his arm earlier say, 'Slut !' I just laughed and strutted on out the door and said, 'Jealous!"

"Grandma, what does slut mean?" Nina asked

"Oh, that's what they call women who have no morals. She sleeps around with a lot of men . That was me. The name suited me then, but not now.

"Anyway, when we got outside, we went to his car. At first we stood by his car and he began kissing on me. I let him and returned his kisses. Before the night was over, we ended up in the backseat of his car. After that night, we became an item. Every weekend we were together. We went to movies and for drives. He always had money. I liked that about him. As I spent time with him, I began to notice that he had a temper. He never showed any hostility toward me, however. But once when someone opened their car door against his, he got so mad he wanted to fight. If the guy hadn't walked away, he would have fought him. Then another time a guy called to me, 'Hey, baby. You're looking good!' Oh, Jake didn't like that at all. When you were with Jake, you were all his. The guy was in a car. We got into his car, and Jake tried to catch up with him. I'm glad he had a good head start on us. I didn't like that about him, but he always treated me good. Also, I felt kind of good that he was willing to fight over me. That was a silly thought as I think of it now. Anyway, I liked him, and I thought he liked me. I felt safe with him, and I knew he wouldn't let anything or anyone hurt me. I had no desire to talk to other men while I had Jake. If someone had told me he would do to me what he did, I would never have believed it. Not Jake. He was such a nice guy, or so I thought.

"Jake had been coming over to my apartment and spending weekends with me for months. I liked that. I had him all to myself and I knew where he was. Valjean had a boyfriend that spent weekend with her too. Like I told you, we shared an apartment together, Valjean and I. It happened one Saturday. Valjean and I had gone shopping for something special to wear to the club that night. We had heard of a new place, and we wanted to look good when we walked in on the arms of our men. You know I had to look good if I was going to walk in on Jake's arm. Like I told you, when he got dressed in his duds, he was one handsome man. I didn't want him to shine all by himself.

"I didn't have very much money, but Jake did. I

would have asked him for some, but he was still asleep when it was time for us to leave. He had put his wallet on the nightstand by the bed. I didn't bother to wake him to ask him if I could have some money. Instead, I went into his wallet and took $20. I figured he wouldn't mind since we were on such good terms. Even if he got mad, I thought I could just sweet talk him into submission just like I had always done with the other men when I wanted to have my way. I'd promise them anything they wanted and things would be okay. But I was wrong. Boy was I wrong! I've never seen a man so angry before. I should have gotten the message by his previous actions that said-'Don't mess with Jake's stuff.' But I was so brazen and self-assured about everything that I ignored the danger signs. That was a fatal mistake. Now I bear the scars of that fatal mistake."

"Ah, Grandma what happened?" Nina asked, mesmerized by every word that was coming out of Essie Mae's mouth.

"Valjean and I caught a ride to town and did our shopping. We had fun talking about our men and about other women and how they acted. We went from store to store until I found the perfect out fit. It was a red polyester pantsuit. The slacks hugged my hips, and the jacket was waist-length. It was low cut so that my cleavage showed. Oh, I was going to make a statement when I walked into that club on Jake's arm, I thought. I had gotten my hair fixed (as we called it then). Everything was ready for Saturday night. At about

8:00 I was dressed and sitting in the kitchen waiting for Jake to come in and tell me how good I looked.

He came in all right. He came in yelling!

"Nina, I'm going to use the language he used just so you can get the real feel of how angry Jake was. You know I don't talk like that, and I better not hear you talking like that either. Do you hear me, Child?"

"Yes, Grandma. I promise I won't."

Essie Mae continued, "Jake was really mad when he came into the kitchen.

"Where is my damn money? Who took my damn money?'

"I took $20 this morning, Honey, to go shopping,' I said ever so sweetly.

"Who told you to take my money? Did I tell you to take my money?"

"No. But I didn't think you would mind, Honey.'

"Well, I do mind. Where is my damn money?'

"I'm wearing it,' I said, turning around so he could get a full view. 'How do you like it?'

"I want my money. Take it off and get me my money,' he insisted.

"Ah, honey, don't be mad,' I said, moving up to him to hug him and to give him a kiss-to charm him like I thought I could do to calm him down. He knocked my arms away and moved to the other side of the room.

"Slut, you better take them clothes off and go back and get my money or I'll...'

"He started to get mad now. I was expecting a whole different reaction and now he was calling me names.

"Or you will do what?' I came back at him.

"I'll tear them off you,' he said and started toward me. The butcher knife was on the kitchen counter, and I grabbed it and said, 'If you touch me, it will be the last thing you ever do.' I held the knife and looked him in the eye. We held the stare for a minute. He believed I was serious, but I don't think I could have cut him if he had called my bluff. He backed off, and I put the knife down. I sat in one of the chairs to let my legs stop shaking. Jake was still mad. He still didn't have his money.

"I want my damn money,' he said. "If you..."

Knock, knock, knock.

Someone was at Essie Mae's door. Just when the story was getting interesting, there was a knock at the door. Nina couldn't believe someone would come to the door at that moment. "Go see who's at the door, Baby, I'll wait until you get back," Essie Mae said. Nina ran as fast as she could, thinking she would get rid of whoever it was in a hurry. She went back to the sunroom where Essie Mae was with a box in her hands. "It was the mailman," she said. "We'll open it later, right, Grandma?" Essie Mae agreed and began the story again.

"I want my damn money,' Jake said. 'Are you going to give it to me?'

"I don't have $20,' I said. 'And I'm not taking this pantsuit back.'

"I should have remembered how he always liked to

get even and not let anyone get over on him. I should have done what he said and took the pantsuit back. But I sat there like a typical woman, disappointed, with her feelings hurt, waiting for him to apologize. He had no intentions of apologizing. Before I knew it, he had the can of cigarette lighter fluid that was sitting on the table and began squirting it all over me, mostly my upper body.

"If you are not going to take it back, then you will not wear it anywhere with me or anyone else.' He tossed the empty can at me and said, 'I'll see you around, slut,' and walked toward the door. At the door, he took his cigarette and flicked it at me and it landed right down my cleavage. Immediately the lighter fluid caught fire. I was in flames by the time Valjean and her boyfriend came out of their room at the sound of my screams. Polyester clings to you when it burns, and when they threw a blanket on me to put out the fire, the pantsuit stuck to my skin.

"Call the ambulance. Call the ambulance,' I could hear someone saying just before I passed out. I woke up in the hospital in excruciating pain. They were cutting the clothes off me. I was screaming at the top of my lungs until they gave me something to put me to sleep. Baby, you don't know how much I suffered during that ordeal. Every time they did something, it hurt and I screamed. I wanted to die. I'm prayed to die. I developed an infection, and they thought I was going to die. I believe I would have died had it not been for Mama's prayers. I called out for Mama. I begged for my mama. I pleaded for my mama. Here I am a grown woman crying for her mama. 'Mama, Mama, come help me. Help me Mama, please,' I begged. As a little girl, I always remembered that Mama could always make things better. She always knew what to do. God always answered her prayers. I hadn't seen Mama in over a year, but I wanted her with me then. I needed help."

Nina's tender heart was breaking from Essie Mae's pain. She couldn't hold back the tears. Essie Mae's vivid memory of the incident caused her to cry too. For a moment they sat in silent tears. Shortly, Essie Mae wiped her eyes, took a deep breath, and continued her story.

"Somehow word got to Mama that I could be dying. One day through severe pain and screams, I heard her call my name. I thought I was dreaming. I opened my eyes and she was there crying at the sight of me. Only my lower body was covered, which didn't get burned that much. I was a terrible sight. Where others turned away when they saw me, Mama didn't. Even my best friend Valjean couldn't stand the sight of me. "Mama, Mama,' was all I could whisper. She didn't fuss at me or say I told you so. She didn't have to because through all the pain, I could remember her saying, 'Essie Mae, why don't you straighten up and start going to church before something bad happens to you?' I didn't listen, and there I lay all burned and suffering, begging for Mama's prayers.

Mama began rubbing my legs and feet, the only area not burned, and she bombarded heaven. *'Lord,'* she said, *'save my daughter. Take away the awful pain she's in. Forgive her for her sinful ways. She needs you now, Lord. Heal her so she can live for you.* "She would pray a while and hum a while. Soon the pain subsided and I drifted off to sleep. That was the first time I slept without heavy doses of painkillers. The next day the infection started clearing up, and I started on the road to recovery. Mama came a few more times to see me. It was a long hospital stay with different treatments and skin grafts. Eventually I was able to go home. For weeks I used to burst out in tears when I looked at myself in the mirror, knowing I would look like that for the rest of my life. Gradually I got used to them and learned how to buy clothes that would cover most of them. So Nina, baby, that's how I got my scars. That's how I got my outer scars. Maybe later I'll tell you how I got my inner scars," Essie Mae said softly.

"What a horrible story, Grandma. I'm so sorry you had to suffer something so horrible. What happened to Jake? Did he go to jail for doing that to you?"

"I was in the hospital so long and unable to press charges that by the time I was able, that skunk had skipped town. I never knew what happened to him." "Grandma, what did you mean when you said you'd tell me later about your inner scars?"

"It's hard to hide the scars you see on my arms and chest. The scars I hide on the inside are just as bad or worse. I don't think I want to talk about those today. Maybe another day. Right now let's see what we can cook up in the kitchen. It looks like the sky is about to clear. Tomorrow will be another beautiful hot day.

But we don't have to worry, do we Child? We have air conditioning! Thank you, Jesus!" they said in unison.

Essie Mae headed to the kitchen with Nina following.

"Nina, honey," Essie Mae said, "tomorrow I want you to go and visit some of your friends. You have been sitting here two days listening to your old grandma talk. It's time for you to spend some time with people your own age."

That night in bed, Nina ran through her mind the things she heard her grandmother say. She couldn't believe that her beloved great-grandmother had been set on fire by a man because of $20. How could anyone be that mean? She, wondered. How Grandma must have suffered, and yet she's still alive and healthy with only a little arthritis to slow her down. Now she is saying something else just as bad or worse happened to her. What could be worse than being set afire by someone you cared about? Oh, Lord, can I bear to hear the next horrible story, Nina thought. But she knew her curiosity would make her listen. She drifted off to sleep, praying for her great-grandmother and thanking God for bringing her through all the awful things that had happened to her.

Essie Mae rubbed her shoulders, elbows, and fingers with some cream for arthritis just before she got into bed. Her mind searched her heart to find confirmation that she had done the right thing to share her life's story with Nina. Would someone that young be able to understand all the horrible things she had experienced? Would she be able to absorb the truth and not let it affect her in a bad way? Should I, she asked her heart, should I tell her the rest of my story? Essie Mae's heart seemed to say to go forth so that she could demonstrate how good God is. How mighty he is to be able to take a person like her, so wrapped in sin, and purify her, and make her a brand new creature. Her former life will truly be a testimony that others will be able to identify with. She hoped it would give others, who think that they are so deep in sin that there is no hope for them, a new lease on life . She could prove there is hope . She could prove that Jesus can change anyone who desires to be changed. With that thought running through her mind, she drifted off to sleep with the decision to go forth with her story.

CHAPTER 5

The next morning at breakfast, Essie Mae said firmly to Nina, "No storytelling today. Today you go visit your friends. I think I'll go visit Martha Nelson today. I heard she wasn't well. Maybe I'll cook a meal or bake her a pie. I'm not sure what she'll want to eat."

Nina didn't argue and called one of her friends after she finished breakfast. Before long she was out the door. Essie Mae gathered some vegetables from the garden, washed them, and put them in a basket to take to Martha. Around 11:30, Essie Mae knocked on Martha's door. She heard a weak, "Come in."

"Martha, honey. How are you?" Essie Mae said in her most caring voice. "I brought you some vegetables from my garden. I hope you'll like them."

She said, "I get so lonely here by myself all the day. You are an angel to come visit a poor old lonely woman like me."

Essie Mae could see how very weak she was and decided to cook her a meal.

"I don't have an appetite for anything. I just don't feel good," she complained. "I went to the doctor and he ran all sorts of tests. I'm supposed to go back for the results tomorrow."

Essie Mae felt compassion for Martha having to live alone. Her daughter came by on a daily basis, but she spent so much time by herself. She was active in church and was a prayer warrior, Essie Mae knew, and didn't mind being alone as long as she could get out and visit. But being so sick lately, all she could do was drag herself out of bed and into her chair each day. Before she became sick, if Essie Mae needed someone to agree with her in prayer about a problem, she knew she could always count on Martha to help her pray the problem through. Essie Mae said, "Martha, you've been sick too long. It's time for you to get healed. You have too much work to do.

"Martha, let's pray and ask God to heal you. You believe God can heal you, don't you?" Essie Mae said.

"Of course I do," Martha said quickly

"Let's pray then," Essie Mae said.

She went and stooped beside Martha's chair and took her hand. Essie Mae bowed her head and closed her eyes and shut out every thought except the thought of the loving Heavenly Father and his precious son, Jesus, who came and died on the cross for the sins of the world. She asked him to forgive her for all her sins and for all Martha's sins. Then she invited Jesus to come into their midst. She reminded him that he said if any two that would touch and agree about anything on earth, he would do it for them (Matt.18:19). Then she prayed for total healing of Martha's condition. It wasn't a long prayer, but it was a prayer full of faith and expectancy. They said amen and went back to their small chatter. Essie Mae noticed that Martha was nodding. She let her sleep and went into the kitchen and began cooking the vegetables she had brought.

Before long, the aroma of biscuits, okra, and fried chicken was floating through the house and out of the open window. Martha awoke feeling hunger pangs, something she hadn't felt in weeks. Essie Mae fixed her plate with just a small amount of okra, one biscuit, one small chicken wing, and a dab of mashed potatoes, and gravy.

"What are you trying to do, starve me to death? Put more food on that plate than that," she said playfully. "Child, I'm hungry enough to eat two chickens!"

Essie Mae laughed and added more food to the plate. "Is this the same weak woman that I prayed for an hour ago?" Essie Mae said in a shocked tone.

"You prayed, didn't you? What did you expect?" God has healed me just that quick. Now let's eat before I die of starvation!" she laughed.

They ate and talked about the goodness of the Lord. Martha shared that her doctor had suspected a tumor in her stomach. She couldn't wait to tell her doctor that Jesus had healed her. She knew what he would say, "Now, now, Ms. Martha, there you go talking nonsense again."

"When he take more x-rays and find nothing, he'll see. He can call it nonsense all he want, but we know better, don't we, Essie Mae? Jesus has healed me! Hallelujah!" Martha said in a loud, strong voice. Essie Mae joined Martha in the high praise.

Essie Mae was so happy she was able to bless Martha in that way. Her visit took her mind off her life's story. Now that the memory door was opened, she had to fight hard to keep them from overwhelming her. When memories rose up to control her mind, she quickly started praising the Lord, if no one was nearby for her to talk to.

"Hey, Grandma. What did you do today?" Nina asked as she breezed into the house around 5:00 with a satisfied look on her face.

"Looks like you had a fun day. What did you do?" Essie Mae asked as she watched Nina flop on the couch.

"Not much. A bunch of us girls had fun watching and teasing the boys as they played softball, that's all. What did you do, Grandma?"

Essie Mae told her all about how she found Martha in such terrible shape and how she prayed for her and cooked for her and how the Lord blessed her.

"Grandma Essie, you do such wonderful things for people. I think the whole world should know how wonderful you are," Nina said, giving her grandmother a kiss.

At the dinner table Nina brought up the idea of

letting the world know how wonderful her grandma was-if not the world, at least the city.

"Grandma, I've been thinking about something."

"What's that, honey?"

"We should have an 'Essie Mae Day' at church one Sunday."

"Ah, Child, don't even think of something like that. I'm nobody special. I just want to please the Lord.

I don't need any praise for that. All the praise I want is from Jesus when I see him face to face."

"Oh come on, Grandma, I want to do this for you. I'll get Mama to help me. I'll talk to the pastor and everything. I think it would be fun."

"I don't know about all that," Essie Mae said. She was thinking if she knew the whole story, she might not want to have such a thing as an" Essie Mae Day."

"When the family comes on Sunday, I will ask them what they think about my suggestion. Is that okay, Grandma?"

Essie Mae relented, seeing that Nina was so excited about the idea. She didn't have the heart to say no and put out that bright light that was shining in those beautiful eyes. Thus, she decided not to tell the rest of her story until she learned the outcome of her survey with the family on Sunday.

Nina got mixed reactions from the family. Some thought it was a wonderful idea, and some thought it would be too much work to pull off, and some even thought no one would be interested in attending such an event. But that didn't stop Nina. She got three or four who said they would be willing to help her. That was enough for her to go forward with her plan. She pinned the four of them down to set a date to meet and start planning. They reminded her that something like that couldn't happen overnight. This she understood, but she didn't want it to be several months either. It was July and she was hoping it could happen by September, at least. The first thing she planned to do was to speak with the Reverend Sykes, the pastor of True Victory Church where the family faithfully attended on Sundays, where Essie Mae was a deaconess and a member of several committees. She was called the "Mother of the church" since she had been a member for so many years and she took an interest in everyone and everything. Reverend Sykes valued her opinion on important matters. It was a small church, holding about one hundred people when packed. The only time it was packed was during a funeral of a popular person or at homecoming when other churches came to worship with True Victory and dinner was served.

Nina's first plan of action was to pay a visit to Reverend Sykes, who she believed would give his full support, and then take it from there.

CHAPTER 6

When Nina awoke on the second Sunday morning in September, the date chosen for "Essie Mae Day," the sun was shining bright. Nina said, "Thank you, Lord." She wanted the day to be perfect. She and her helpers had worked very hard to get to that day. They had arranged for Essie Mae's favorite male chorus to sing and arranged a food committee to set out the food. They would eat outside under the trees just like in the olden days when churches didn't have fellowship halls. With the sun shining and the weather nice and warm, it promised to be a perfect day. The special day had been announced for several Sundays, and everyone was invited to attend. Nina had come up with the idea of having a "Money Tree" as a special gift for Essie Mae. All the money would be placed on the tree created by Nina. Essie Mae could do whatever she wished with the money. But knowing her as Nina did, most of the money would be donated or given to someone in need. To get the other women involved, Nina decided to have a hat contest. All the older women in True Victory sported hats of all shapes and sizes at every church function. Even Essie Mae thought she wasn't dressed if she didn't have a hat to match her outfit.

Nina tingled with excitement all through the morning service in anticipation of the afternoon program just for her grandmother.

After the morning service, very few people left, but others kept coming in until the church was "packed." Nina was elated. Knowing that food would be served afterward was a great incentive for some who stayed. But that was okay with Nina as long as the church was full. Nina acted as mistress of ceremony. At 2:00, Reverend Sykes turned the program over to her. Her mom and aunts, her support group, sat to the side to give her encouragement. The male chorus sang their hearts out, bringing everyone to their feet.

Nina had a segment where different ones took turns to tell what Essie Mae had done for them and how much they loved her. "She's just an angel," was heard over and over again from several people. Martha told of how Essie Mae came to her rescue when she was so very sick and she came and prayed for her and God healed her and then she cooked her "the best meal she ever had." Essie Mae's oldest and dearest friend, Valjean, was able to attend. This made Nina the happiest because at first it seemed like she wouldn't since she lived in another state. She came in during the hat contest. Nina had called each lady to the front who wanted to participate in the contest. There were about ten ladies, including Essie Mae. Essie Mae had shopped for days trying to find the perfect hat for her perfect outfit. The ladies smiled and pranced around-each doing their own little thing to bring attention to themselves. The congregation roared with laughter. The more they laughed, the more the ladies put on. To judge, Nina had the congregation clap for the one they thought wore the fanciest hat. At the end, each lady got a small gift. There was no way it could be said that one lady's hat looked better than another. Who wanted to start a rivalry in the church? Not Nina. She had asked the congregation to give the ladies another round of applause when Valjean walked in. When Essie Mae saw her, they both ran into each other's arms for a long embrace. When they finally let go, Valjean, wiping her eyes, wanted to say a few words. She had a lot of wonderful things to say about her oldest and dearest friend. She wanted to tell about a funny experience they had together as young converts wanting to go out and save the whole town. Before long, she had the whole congregation roaring with laughter.

"I bet Essie Mae never told you all this story, did she?" Valjean began. "Essie Mae hounded me into getting saved. She got saved first, and I thought she would drive me crazy if I didn't say yes and pray the sinner's prayer. I know now she did it because she loved me. I would probably be dead and in hell now if she hadn't been so persistent, because I was in bad shape. Anyway, after I got saved, we became inseparable like we were when we were living for the devil. Except now we were living for the Lord. Every Saturday we'd go to different neighborhoods knocking on doors asking if they knew Jesus. We were on fire for the Lord and wanted everyone to have what we had. With our Bibles in our arms, comfortable shoes on, and the Holy Ghost in us, we hit the streets armed for battle. Some laughed at us and called us holy rollers, some ran when they saw us coming, and yet some were hungry and accepted the Word. One Saturday we decided to go into this new neighborhood. We approached this one house and we heard this mean-sounding dog barking. We stopped in our tracks. Suddenly, from around the house here comes this dog. I grabbed Essie Mae's arm and said, 'Run!' We took off running. The dog came after us. He had this menacing sounding bark that if he caught you, he would tear you to pieces. We drew a lot of attention on that street. People stood on their porches and laughed. No one offered to help us. That we couldn't understand. We even yelled, 'Help us.' Nobody offered-they just laughed. The dog was gaining on us and we were getting tired. Essie Mae said, 'What's wrong with us? We're running from a dog with our Bibles in our hands. What kind of example are we giving the people? We got the Holy Ghost, why are we running from a dog? Do you have faith to stop and face this dog?' Essie Mae has always been braver than me," Valjean added. "I told her, 'I don't think we have a choice, because I am too tired to run any further.' So we stopped and turned around quickly and in between gasping for air, Essie Mae pointed her finger at that dog and said, 'Stop. I command you to stop in Jesus' name.' The dog stopped and barked a few more times, turned, and slowly ran the opposite direction. Essie Mae and I looked at each other and burst out laughing. We sat on the curb and laughed until our sides hurt. Then we understood why everyone else was laughing. Do you know why? The dog had no teeth! We were running from a toothless dog!

The congregation roared with laughter. Nina hadn't heard that story before.

After she spoke, Valjean gave Essie Mae another warm embrace and tiptoed out. She had a speaking engagement on the other side of town.

Valjean was the last speaker. The program was winding down. Essie Mae had been presented with a large bouquet of red roses. She had given a short speech thanking everyone for their kindness and attendance and how overjoyed she was to see her best friend Valjean. She was especially pleased with the "Money Tree." "Who said money don't grow on trees?" she joked. She raved highly of Nina and her loving family. Mostly, she honored God and gave a short sermon on living a life of righteousness, forgiveness, and love. She had to do it. How could she let such an opportunity go by? She kept it short, knowing there was food waiting out under the shade trees of the church. Expressing her joy for being honored in such a way brought her to tears. She exclaimed,

"This is one of the happiest days of my life. Thank you all for being a part of it."

As Nina was drawing the program to a close, she

was about to say, "If all hearts are clear, we will have a closing prayer by pastor Sykes." Just after she said, "If all hearts are clear," a voice in the back of the church said, "Please forgive me, but I would like to say something." Everyone turned around trying to see whose voice they were hearing. They didn't want to hear anyone else speak. They were ready to go outside and eat some good fried chicken and potato salad. Everyone whispered, "Who is that?" No one seemed to recognize him. He was a total stranger to True Victory Church. The stranger slowly made his way up the aisle to the front of the church. He was dressed in baggy pants, a shirt that was white once, no jacket, and no tie. His hair was gray and needed combing. His shoes were worn over and worn out. As he took a step, his shoes dragged the floor. He fumbled his worn hat nervously in both his hands. His head hung low and his face was creased with wrinkles, and he needed a shave.

"Please forgive me," he repeated in a raspy voice. "I just have to get this off my chest before I die. I heard the church was a place for repenting, and that's why I'm here today, to repent."

He had the entire congregation's attention now. They had forgotten the fried chicken and potato salad. They were about to get something they enjoyed better – hearing about someone else's sin; something they could talk about for days. The stranger had a hundred pairs of eyes glued on him, including Essie Mae's. However, Essie Mae had a look of horror on her face. "I'm sorry to interrupt your service today," the stranger said slowly.

"But something brought me to this church today. I ain't been in a church for years, even though my mama used to take me when I was young. But when I got up to be grown, at least I thought I was grown, I decided I didn't need church no mo'. Now I realize I made the biggest mistake of my life. The next biggest mistake is what brought me here today. I need to ask forgiveness to a person in this church. I don't have to call that person by name. I did an awful thing to them a long time ago. I can't go to my grave without saying how sorry I am and if they can find it in their heart to forgive me."

The strange, unkempt man kept his head down and looked at the floor the whole time he spoke, all the while fidgeting with his hat. When he finished, he continued to look down and slowly shuffled down the aisle and out the door. No one said a word. You could have heard the church mouse squeak. Everyone was that quiet. Essie Mae's head was down now too, and her eyes were moist with tears. The question on everyone mind was, "Who was this man, and who was he apologizing to?" They would ask Deacon Bob, who seemed to know everybody in town.

Nina broke the silence by announcing that the service was over and the pastor would give the closing prayer. The people slowly strolled out to the back of the church where the food had been spread on several large tables placed end-to-end with white tablecloths covering them. Food covered every inch of the tables: fried chicken, potato salad, string beans and corn, casseroles, cakes, and pies of all kind. The people lined up from one end to the other, piling up their plates. This was the kind of spread they loved. Everyone was laughing, joking, and eating, and having a wonderful time.

This was exactly how Nina dreamed it would be.

Essie Mae's heart was overjoyed to see everyone enjoying themselves. *What a perfect day!* she thought. She glanced at the very end of the tables and saw a man sitting there alone. She wondered why he wasn't up getting his food. Then she saw Deacon Bob hand him a plate. Essie Mae headed toward them. About halfway there she noticed it was the unkempt man that had just left the church. *I might have known, she thought to herself, that Deacon Bob would be the first to extend a welcoming hand. He is known for his mission to reach the downtrodden. Then she thought, Should I pretend I don't recognize him or should I grant him his request? Lord, this is one of the hardest things I have ever been faced with. Something I never thought I would ever have to do.* How dare he come and disrupt my special day. Here he is begging for forgiveness after what he did to me. He wants me to tell him I forgive him? That was something I never thought I would have to do. Essie Mae couldn't understand the agony she was going through. She thought she had gotten rid of all the hateful feelings shortly after she got saved. She hadn't thought of him or the accident in many years. Why was the sight of him causing her to go through such turmoil? Why wasn't it easy for her to walk up to him and say those precious three word, I forgive you? Maybe it would have been easier if she had not so recently told the story to Nina, the memories of the pain of her flesh being ripped from her body as the doctors removed the clothes that had melted to her from being set on fire. *Oh God, I know I must face him, but you are going to have to give me strength,* Essie Mae prayed.

No one seemed to notice the turmoil Essie Mae was going through at that moment. Each step she took her legs and feet got heavier and heavier and her heart pounded with anxiety. Nina noticed Essie Mae heading toward the man, but she thought she was going to greet him to make him feel welcomed. Little did she know that Essie Mae was making the journey of a lifetime. For a brief second inside the church when the unkempt man started to speak, a flashback of pain shot through her body that almost took her breath away. It took every ounce of strength she had not to get up and run out of the church as he spoke, but she didn't want to draw attention to herself. She had never in her life been so relieved as she was when the man stopped speaking and shuffled out of the church, never to be seen again at least that's what she thought. But now she was heading toward him to say the words he pitifully begged for inside the church.

Essie Mae often wondered how she would react if she every saw the man who flicked that fatal cigarette butt and walked away. She used to dream of killing him in several different ways such as, running him over with a car, throwing lye in his face to let him see how it felt, or to stab him in his heart and watch him bleed to death. But those thoughts were from the old

Essie Mae. The sinful Essie Mae that wanted revenge for all the pain and embarrassment she'd endured. But this was the new Essie Mae, the spirit-filled and born-again Essie Mae that is struggling to get to him at that moment. When she got saved and the preacher preached you must forgive everyone who has wronged you, she purposed in her heart to forgive everyone, even him. Which was somewhat easy since she didn't have to lay eyes on him ever again, she thought. But now she was nearly face to face with that... No she couldn't call him a name. She must be respectful. She stood about five paces in front of him and cleared her voice. He looked up into her face and immediately placed his plate on the ground and stood up.

"I've come to say ... I-I forgive you," Essie Mae said slowly.

He looked into her eyes and tears started rolling down his cheeks. He dropped his head and softly said, "Thank you. This means more than you ever know."

Essie Mae may not have heard his heartfelt thanks because when the man dropped his head, Essie Mae turned and walked away as quickly as her legs would carry her. She didn't look back. She headed back to the church and sat in one of the pews and sobbed and asked the Lord to forgive her for being so weak. *If I have the love of Jesus in my heart, why was it so hard to forgive Jake?* Jake, the man who gave her the scars she'd carry for the rest of her life. No one would understand why she was reacting that way. The majority of people who knew her story would say that it's understandable to hate the person who had caused her so much pain. Some would never forgive him. But Essie Mae reasoned, didn't Jesus forgive those who beat him all night long-using a whip with metal tips to rip out the flesh from his back at each strike? Didn't he forgive them who put a thorn wreath with sharp needles on his head and pushed it deep into his skull? He forgave those Roman soldiers who made him carry his cross up the hill and nailed his hands and feet to the cross and shoved a spear into his side while he hung there in agony. What was his word to the Father?" Forgive them!" After all that, he loved them still and forgave them.

"Oh Father, forgive me and help me to love like you love. You have forgiven me of so many sins.

Surely, it should have been easier for me to forgive Jake."

As the tears stopped coming, Essie Mae felt a cleansing and a burden being lifted from her. Suddenly, she felt a presence near her. She slowly lifted her head from her arm and looked up to see Jake standing looking down at her. She wiped her eyes and stood facing him.

"Excuse me for intruding," he said slowly. "I just wanted you to know that I didn't come here to cause you anymore pain. I came because I was compelled to come. I knew you never wanted to see me again. I don't blame you after what I did. I was an awful person back then. I had plenty of time to think of all the terrible things I had done to people when I got sent to prison for twenty years for shooting a man. As I looked back on my life while in prison, I realized I must have been possessed. I can't believe I did that to you and just walked away. Your screams haunted me for years. But while I was in prison, I started going to a little Bible study and started listening to preaching on the radio. I eventually surrendered my life to Jesus. I've only been out of prison for a couple of months. I don't have clothes for church, but I saw a flyer about you being honored today and I was compelled to come and make my plea for forgiveness. I believe the Lord compelled me. I have asked him over and over to forgive me for what I did to you. With you actually saying, 'I forgive you,' I believe I have been forgiven. It's like the Lord said it to me today, 'I forgive you, Jake.' Now I feel like a burden has been lifted and now I can go on and live the rest of my life, however long that is, trying to do good. Thank you, Essie Mae. Good-bye."

"It seems God has lifted two burdens today," Essie Mae said when she finally spoke. "Good-bye, Jake," she said and reached out her arms and gave him a gentle embrace. With moist eyes, he turned and shuffled out of the church, down the steps, and headed toward the bus stop. She watched him go and wondered where would he go, what would he do? He seemed so alone, except for the knowledge of Jesus. Essie Mae whispered a soft prayer asking the Lord to be with Jake.

As Essie Mae dried her eyes and prepared to rejoin the group outside, Nina rushed in.

"Grandma Essie, we were looking for you. Who was that man? Why was he in here talking to you? What did he want?"

"Slow down, Child. One question at a time. I'll tell you later. But now I must get back to my company. I've been in here too long. They might think I'm being anti-social. Come on. I'm starving. I hope they left me some food."

"Ah, Grandma, there's plenty of food." Essie Mae took Nina's hand and headed back to the churchyard.

At home that night, Nina counted the money Essie Mae got on her money tree.

"Grandma, you have $300. What are you going to do with all this money?"

"I don't know. I'll probably put it away for a rainy day."

"You could buy a lot of hats with this money."

"Maybe one. But I'm going to save most of it. You never know when an emergency might come."

Essie Mae took the money and handed Nina fifty dollars. "This is for you. You can buy you something new for school. You are such a wonderful child, and I love you very much. You worked so hard for your dear old grandma. And I sure do appreciate it. It's been a wonderful day. Now I'm going to bed, I'm kinda tired."

Essie Mae kissed Nina good night and went into her bedroom. Nina went to her room. She got into bed and let the memories of the day flow through her mind. The group sang all the songs her grandmother liked, and the hat contest made her smile as she remembered the older women trying to strut and look sexy in their fancy hats. The money made her the most proud. She never expected that much. The food was tasty and plentiful. Yes, everything went well, she thought. The people showed up-the church was full. The funny story Valjean told made everyone laugh. Nina was proud of herself and glad she was able to do that for someone who was so dear to her. One little incident nagged at her memory. Who was that tattered old man who came to ask for forgiveness? I must ask Grandma tomorrow, she thought as she drifted off.

Essie Mae felt extremely tired as she prepared for bed. She couldn't remember ever being that tired. She normally had lots of energy. She got fatigued, but never like she felt then. The encounter with Jake came to her mind. The stress of seeing him is probably what zapped her energy. She never thought she would ever see him again, and in he walks on one of the happiest days of her life. Now she has forgiven him, hopefully she can forget him. I'll have to tell Nina who he was. She will want to know, she thought. Oh, God help me. She took a deep breath and it seemed her heart raced faster. Then it seemed like she wasn't getting enough air. She needed help! She tried to call out for Nina, but her voice was barely above a whisper, which a sleeping Nina could not hear. She continued to gasp for air. She reached for the phone on the night stand, but it slipped from her hand and fell to the floor. Help me, Je sus, she tried to say.

Nina was now in dreamland. She had no trouble falling to sleep. In the dream someone was calling her name. She heard, "Wake up Nina." She struggled to awake, but she couldn't. "Wake up, Nina," the voice came again with urgency. Then she felt someone slap her on her thigh. It was a burning slap and she woke with a jolt. She setup in bed and in the darkness of her room and rubbed her painful thigh. What a strange dream, she thought. She decided to get up and go see if Essie Mae had tried to wake her. When she got to the door, she gently tapped and softly called, "Grandma, did you call me?" She slowly pushed the door open and stepped into the room. She heard Essie Mae gasping for air. She turned on the light and could see that Essie Mae. was not well. "Call the doctor," Essie Mac managed to say. Nina's heart began to pound. She didn't know what doctor to call. With shaky fingers she dialed her mother's number. "Mama, something's wrong with Grandma!" she managed to say without screaming. "She can't breathe."

"I'll be right over, Nina, honey," her mother said. "Stay with her and fan her." She could tell how excited Nina was. Nina was a level-headed girl, but she had never seen her grandmother sick before. Nina held Essie Mae's hand with one hand and fanned with the other. She also prayed, Lord don't let my grandmother die.

Essie Mae didn't die. The doctor said she had had a mild heart attack and if she took it easy she should recover fully. She shouldn't be under much stress. Essie Mae's family promised to help her recover, especially Nina, who everyone believed saved her grandma's life. Nina would think often, What if I hadn't awakened? And then she'd think, How did I wake up? How can you dream someone has hit you and you wake up with pain exactly where you dreamed you were hit? That was truly a mystery to her. She would have to discuss that with her grandma during one of their talks. She was glad that there would be many more opportunities to have those talks. She thanked the Lord for answering her prayer not to let her grandma die.

CHAPTER 7

Essie Mae recovered completely. She had resumed her activities with the church and visiting the sick. She was able to attend Nina's high school graduation a year later. She beamed as Nina gave the Valedictorian speech. That washer baby up there, and she told everyone who would listen, especially when her name was mentioned. Her name was among those Nina listed who had been a great influence in her life. God was number one and she was number two. She didn't hear any of the other names Nina had listed because hearing her own name blocked out all the others. That was a proud moment for Essie Mae. In the fall, Nina went off to college. What a bittersweet day that was for the whole family.

Now Nina was home for the summer and she was visiting Essie Mae and they sat on the porch in the midst of a cool breeze and chatted. It was much like the summer they sat on that same porch two years ago in the welting heat waiting for the air conditioning unit to arrive when Essie Mae began telling her life's story. The memory crossed both their minds. "Grandma, do you believe in angels?" Nina asked

"Yes I do. Why do you ask, Child?"

"Well, I have often wondered if an angel woke me up the night you got sick."

"What happened the night I got sick? I remember how brave you were. I have thanked the Lord a thousand times for letting you be there that night."

"You see, I was in a deep sleep and I was dreaming. I could hear someone telling me to wake up, but I couldn't wake up no matter how I tried. Whoever that person was hit me on my right thigh, and I woke up with a jolt and my right thigh was stinging from that slap. That's when I came to your room and found you sick. I often wondered if an angel hit me and woke me up," Nina said.

When Nina looked at Essie Mae, she saw a strange look on her face.

"Grandma, what's wrong?"

"Maybe it was an angel that woke you, Child," she said remembering another desperate time when she needed an angel and one suddenly appeared.

"I believe I have seen my guardian angel. I know she exists," Essie Mae said with conviction. "I haven't told anyone about it because people tend to make fun of you when you start talking of spiritual things. But I thank God for my guardian angel. She has come to my rescue lots of times."

"Grandma, tell me about her. What did she look

like? How did you know she was an angel?" Nina asked excitedly.

"Baby, the story behind it isn't pretty. Actually, it's the one I'd rather not recall. To tell you about her, I would have to tell you the rest of my life's story. You remember the summer I told you about how I got my scars and I said the scars I hide on the inside are just as bad or worse? In order for me to tell you about my guardian angel, I will have to expose those inner scars to you."

"Do you want to do that, Grandma? If you think it's too painful, then don't bother to tell me. Remember, you're not supposed to be under a lot of stress. I often wonder if seeing Jake that day brought on the heart attack you had. So don't tell me anymore about your life if you think bringing up old memories might bring pressure on your heart," Nina said.

"Maybe the Lord spared me and healed me so I could tell you the rest of the story. I believe I'm supposed to tell you. I've prepared myself by praying and strengthening my spirit. I have your tape recorder in my bedroom just waiting for this moment. So go on in and get it and let's get started, Child."

"Okay, Grandma, if you're sure." Nina was excited to learn more about Essie Mae's guardian angel, yet she was a little apprehensive about Essie Mae's reaction to dredging up those bad memories she had buried so deeply for so many years. She hurried to get the tape recorder. She noticed the new blank tapes sitting on top of the recorder. That let Nina know that Grandma was serious and ready to tell her the story. But she stopped a minute and said a quick prayer, "Dear Lord, don't let anything happen to my grandma after telling this story."

"Okay, Grandma, I'm ready," Nina said after returning to the porch.

"All right, then, let's get started," Essie Mae said and began to tell her story. "After I got burned and the doctors turned me loose saying that this," she said, pointing to the scars, "was the best they could do for me, I sat home for over a year barely going anywhere. Now and then I'd go see Mama and Daddy. Mama would hug me tight and tell me she still loved me. She encouraged me to start attending church. I'd go a few times because I promised Mama, but I never made a commitment to the Lord. After a while, my friend Valjean talked me into going with her to a movie. After she saw I handled that okay, she talked me into going to a party. I was so scared someone would take a look at me and laugh and I would be so embarrassed. So I covered most of the scars with clothes and hoped no one would pay any attention to the rest. After taking a few drinks, I didn't care what people thought. Before long, I was back to my old routine-drinking and men. They didn't seem to care about my scars. I was back laughing, drinking, and dancing. My visits to Mama and Daddy stopped. I was having fun again!

"Grandma, how old were you then?"

"I was around thirty-eight years old. I even married one of the fellows I dated. I thought he was the best thing around. He and I liked the same things-having fun and drinking. But after being married for about three years, it was over.

"Grandma, I never knew you were married again. What was his name?"

"It was such a short marriage, hardly anyone remembers his name. His name was Austin Bedford. He sure did know how to party. And dance... Wow! Everybody loved to see him dance. I was always attracted to a man that could dance. We won contests together in the juke-joints we hung out in. You never saw such wiggling and shaking and fancy footwork as you did during these contests. He was the only man that I came close to loving like I loved my first husband, Jocko. That's the only reason I agreed to marry him, I fell in love. I didn't think I would ever get married again. But Austin captured my heart. A little boy was born out of that union. I didn't think I could get pregnant anymore. I guess it was the power of love that did it."

"What?! You mean to tell me I have another cousin somewhere out there?" Nina asked in astonishment.

"No. He died as a teenager. Most of the family didn't know about him. Certainly not Mama and Daddy. Only my children, and Austin, of course.

"When Austin married me and made a respectable woman out of me with so much love and affection, I should have been the happiest woman in the world. But I'd have periods when I became gloomy and sad. The only thing that gave me a lift when I felt that way was alcohol. So we kept beer and whiskey on hand at all times. Sometimes I'd look at the scars on my body and think how I hated the man that did that to me. I'd swear to myself that no man would ever hurt me again and get away with it. That thought stayed with me all the time. If Austin and I rough-housed and it felt like he was getting the best of me, something inside of me would snap and I'd go wild. I frightened him a few times and he got to the point he wouldn't play that way with me. I remember one time we were playing and he had me by the arms, pinned down on the bed. He was on top of me and I couldn't move. Suddenly fear came over me and I drew my legs up under him and bent my knees and with all my might I pushed him and he went flying across the room and bounced off the dresser. It hurt his back and arm. He looked at me with disbelief and horror. For a brief time I sat on the bed huffing and puffing like a mad bull with a scowl on my face. He just kept saying, 'What's the matter with you, baby?' When I calmed down, I was so sorry. I told him so over and over. I got ice for his bruises and held him extra tight that night. But he never played with me again. I don't think we were ever as close as we once were. Suddenly, the things he used to overlook became arguments. We drew further and further apart. A dark cloud seemed to hover over me all the time. I wanted our marriage to work, but I couldn't get out from under that dark cloud no matter how hard I tried." "But Grandma, you had little Austin Jr. Didn't he bring you joy?"

"Baby, it just wasn't enough. Sure I was crazy about Little Austin, AJ we later called him. But when I was in one of my dark moods, even he got scolded a lot.

In today's society, people who go through the type of traumatic experience I went through when I got burned, they would have placed them in some type of counseling. But back then in the forties and fifties you hardly heard of counseling, especially if you were poor. I had to deal with it the best I could. So I buried the pain and pretended I was okay. But I wasn't okay. Drinking and smoking helped me get through each day.

"I remember the day I lost everything," Essie Mae went on. "I was in a drunken stupor lying across the bed when Austin came in carrying AJ, who was about a year old at the time. He had AJ in one arm and a suitcase in the other. He said, 'I'm leaving and I'm taking the baby with me. I can't take this anymore. I'll be at my mother's.' I wanted to get up and run after him and beg him not to go, but I could barely lift my head off the bed. I heard the door slam, and I passed out. When I woke the next day, the apartment was so very, very quiet. I cried all day long. I'd lost all that was dear to me. That was another painful experience I had to learn to live with. After a while, I buried it down with the other stuff and went on with my life. Before too long I had hooked up with another man-more partying, drinking, and smoking. I was once again the life of the party. I laughed and drank so I wouldn't remember my pain.

"After Austin and I broke up, my girlfriend Valjean moved in to share the apartment expenses. We were back together again. What a great pair we were! She liked drinking and partying as much as I did. She changed boyfriends as often as I did. But she never had any that abused her the way I did. I don't know why I attracted that kind. The only good one I had was Austin and I drove him away."

"Grandma, did you ever see little Austin again?" Nina asked.

"Austin tried to arrange for me to see him, but each time he called he could tell I'd been drinking and he wouldn't bother to bring him by. One day Valjean brought me the newspaper and showed me an article about a car crash and a thirteen-year-old boy was killed. He was riding his bike when a car ran out of control and hit him. The driver was drunk. The boy was my son, AJ. I screamed at the top of my lungs... No! No! No! I couldn't believe my baby was dead. Later that day, Austin dropped by to tell me the news. I could tell he'd been crying. He didn't even seem to notice that I'd been drinking. He was so sad. We hugged and cried on each other's shoulders.

"I didn't think I could make it through the funeral without a drink. I didn't drink much, but people could tell I had been drinking. When I walked up to view the body, I heard someone whisper, "There's the mother. She's probably drunk.' I ignored the remark. When I saw my baby lying there so handsome, so very still, I fell to pieces. I burst out bawling... My baby! My baby! I fell over on him and bawled for all the times I wasn't with him, for all the times I didn't hear him say Mama, for all the times I wasn't there to hold him in my arms and say I love you. When the usher finally pulled me away, I was saying, 'I love you, Austin. I love you, son.'

I cried for days. Not just for Little Austin, but for all the pain I'd gone through and pretended wasn't there. Eventually, there were no more tears, and I still had no one to love me. I once again turned to the bottle."

"Oh, Grandma, what a sad, sad story," Nina said and got up and went to Essie Mae and lay her head in her lap. Essie Mae gently stroked her hair. They sat that way for a long time. Nina whispered, "I love you, Grandma."

"I know you do, Honey. And you know Grandma truly loves you."

There was no more story-telling that day. They spent the time cooking and talking about Nina's new friends at college.

That night while lying in bed thinking of all the things her grandmother had said that day, Nina could hardly believe this was her grandmother talking. *How someone could go through as much as she has gone through and be as sweet as she is? God must be real if he can change Grandma from the woman she has been describing into the godly woman she is today, she told herself. She wondered what more Grandma could tell. She must be going to tell me about her conversion when we get together again.* I know that will be some story, Nina thought as she turned out the light and soon drifted off to sleep.

As Nina was drifting off to sleep, Essie Mae placed her Bible on the bedside table after reading several chapters and slipped to her knees and prayed for her family, friends, community, and the world. It took a while to get around to everybody. But she persevered nightly. When she finally got into bed, instead of going to sleep, she thought about where the story of her life would lead when she and Nina talked next. She was leading up to the most dreadful time of her life. However painful it might be, to her and to Nina, she was determined to get the whole horrendous story out. "Oh God," she whispered. "Help me get through this." After tossing and turning for a while, she finally drifted off to sleep.

CHAPTER 8

The sun was bright and the birds were chirping when Essie Mae woke early the next morning. After her quiet time with the Lord, she headed for the kitchen to cook breakfast. Everything was just about done when Nina dragged in with sleep still hanging over her.

"Grandma, why do you get up so early?" Nina yawned. We could sleep 'til 9:00. We don't have anywhere to go."

"Baby, I can't stay in bed that long. I guess I'm like my mama. She always had to get up at daybreak to help on the farm. If I sleep later than 6:30 am, I've overslept. Come on, have some of these hot biscuits and jelly. Your eggs and bacon are coming up."

"Grandma, are you going to tell more about your life today?" Nina asked as she munched on the crispy bacon.

"I'd like to if you don't have anywhere to go. But if you do, the story can wait. You should be out having fun anyway, not sitting here listening to an old woman's sinful life's story."

"Oh, Grandma, this is for my book, remember. I'm going to write your life story and everyone will see how God can change a person."

"Today, Baby, I will get to the worst part and tell you about my angel."

"Grandma, I can't imagine anything being worse than what I've already heard," Nina said with a look of bewilderment.

They finished their breakfast, and Nina helped clean the kitchen. At about 10:00 they were both dressed and ready to take their seats out on the porch. Nina carried her tape recorder and Essie Mae her Bible. It was a lovely late-June morning. The sun hadn't heated the air yet, so they enjoyed a comfortable breeze. The grass was green and the buttercups were blooming – yellow, white, and pink. The neighborhood was quiet when Essie Mae eased into her story...

"Like I said, I continued to drink and run around with men. I met this one man ..."

"Hey, Essie Mae. How are you doing this beautiful morning?" came the greeting from across the street. The interruption came from Essie Mae's friend, Lula.

Essie Mae got up and went down the steps to chat with her friend. They chatted for about half an hour before Lula said she had to go. Essie Mae came back to her seat on the porch and said, "Now, where were we?" She was ready to continue the story. By the time they got started again, one of Nina's friends drove up.

"Hey girl, your mother told me you were here. What are you doing?"

"Just sitting here talking to Grandma Essie."

"Come ride me to the new mall. I want to look around and maybe buy some shoes."

"Go on, Nina. You need to have some fun with your friends. You don't need to be stuck up under your old grandma all the time. Get your shoes on and go. We can talk tomorrow."

"You promise, Grandma? I really want to hear the rest of the story." "I promise we will get to the end tomorrow."

Nina ran and got her shoes and purse and hopped in the car with her friend. She waved good-bye. Essie Mae was disappointed and relieved at the same time. She had her mind set to finish her story, yet she was glad she didn't have to say the words out loud just yet.

The phone rang. It was Emma Puckett, president of the Women's Auxiliary. She called to say that there was going to be an emergency meeting at church that night. Essie Mae spent over an hour talking on the phone with Emma. This was good because it kept her mind occupied.

When she got home after the emergency meeting, she continued to ponder over all the plans the women had come up with to raise money to pay for Pastor Sykes' emergency surgery. He had no insurance and the operation must take place soon or he could die. The women were pulling together to raise the $5,000 needed for the operation. They would sell dinners, have a rummage sale, have a cake walk, and sell candy to get started. The Auxiliary would be busy for several months. But with the Lord's help, they knew they would raise enough money to pay Pastor's hospital bills. Essie Mae fell asleep with the Women's Auxiliary plans on her mind and not her life's story for a change. She slept more peacefully than she had in days.

Nina woke to the sound of Essie Mae humming one of her favorites hymns-"Love Lifted Me." It was a comforting sound. She dressed and followed the aroma of hot biscuits to the kitchen where Essie Mae moved joyfully about.

"Good morning, Grandma," Nina said as she sat at the table and sipped her orange juice. "You're in a good mood this morning."

"Good morning, Baby. Yes, I am. God is so good. I woke up with that song ringing in my heart-Love *Lifted Me.'* I tell you, when I was sinking deep in sin, far from the peaceful shore," Essie Mae said, repeating a part of the song, "God's love truly lifted me."

"Did you and your friend have fun yesterday?" Essie Mae asked Nina.

"Yes. And guess what? Cheryl and I put in an application at an ad agency for a summer job. I'll get to show off some of my writing skills if I get the job. They said they needed some reliable help. They thought Cheryl and I looked like two responsible girls. I hope we get the job. I'll be able to buy my clothes for college this fall.

"I'll pray that you and Cheryl get the job. God's

got it all in control." "You and Reverend Sykes always say that, Grandma."

"It's a true statement, Child, and don't ever forget it."

"And speaking of Pastor Sykes, he is very ill and needs an operation," Essie Mae shared. "But he doesn't have any insurance. So the Women's Auxiliary will have several fundraisers until we raise the $5,000 needed. We know we can do it. You know what our motto is don't you? 'We can do all things through Christ who strengthens us.' Do you know that scripture?" Essie Mae asked Nina with a smile.

"Oh, Grandma, that's an easy one. That's Philippians 4:13. Grandma, I'll help with your fundraisers until I get my job," Nina said with confidence.

"Well, I won't get much help out of you then, for I'm sure they will be calling you soon. If they are smart, they'll call you today!" Essie Mae said, giving Nina a big hug. "Now where are we going to sit and finish this story of mine?"

"Let's sit in the sunroom. I love it in there. It's so bright and cheerful. It makes you feel like you are outside, without the heat, bugs, and noise. Also, it is unlikely that we will be disturbed. We can ignore the phone calls and the knocks on the door," Nina said.

"Sunroom it is," said Essie Mae with a little excitement in her voice. Nina didn't hear the usual dread that once haunted Essie Mae when she was preparing to go deeper into her past. What had removed the haunting in her voice Nina didn't know. But she felt a little better about listening to the story with Essie Mae not seeming to dread telling it so.

They both got comfortable in their seats. Essie Mae waited while Nina set up her tape recorder. The sun, shining through the windows, made the room bright and lively as if God was smiling directly down on them. Even the birds' cheerful singing from the trees outside the windows agreed with them that it was a lovely day.

"Grandma, you seem so calm today. You used to have a sense of dread about telling your story. What happened?" Nina asked.

"Jesus has strengthened me," Essie Mae said. "Remember how stressed and weary Jesus was in the Garden of Gethsemane the night before he was to be taken before the religious leaders to start the process of his crucifixion? He was in agony knowing what was about to happen. He was praying asking God to take that cup he was about to drink away, yet he was willing to go through with it if God wanted him to. That story is found in the gospel of Matthew. Can you tell me what chapter?" Essie Mae asked to see if Nina could rattle that one off the tip of her tongue as she had done each time before.

"It's Matthew 26, isn't it?" Nina said hesitantly. Essie Mae smiled in agreement and continued on with the story.

"The Bible said his sweat was like drops of blood. Now you know he was stressed. Then the Bible said an angel came and ministered to him and strengthened him. That's what happened to me. I was stressing out having to tell you this next part of my life and God sent his Holy Spirit to strengthen me. I woke up with a song in my heart. You heard me singing-love lifted me! That song is true for me. *'I was sinking deep in sin, far from the peaceful shore'*... God's love lifted me those many years ago."

"How did God's love lift you, Grandma?"

"Well, Child, let me tell you. I continued to live a wild life. It was so easy for me to live that way. To try to change would have taken too much effort. My girlfriend, Valjean, and I continued to pal around going to clubs and dating different men. When I finally got over Austin, I told myself I would never allow myself to fall in love with another man. So now I had two things I promised myself I would never do. I would never let another man physically hurt me and I would never fall in love again.

"I met Roy one night at some juke joint Valjean and I heard about. Valjean had a steady boyfriend staying with her. He had a car, so we always had transportation. The club wasn't much of a place-a little hole in a wall, the old saying was. It was a small place, so the eight to ten people there made the place look crowded. I noticed Roy right away because he was buying drinks. That was the only reason I noticed him. He was not an attractive guy. However, he was spending money, so I overlooked the part that he was ugly. He also kept the music in the jukebox going. The two things I liked drinks and music. He kept both available to me. We danced a few times, and before I knew it he was clinging to me. The more

I drank, the more I laughed and danced in the most obscene manner-especially the slow songs. You never seen so much rubbing and grinding-nothing between us but clothes. When I was drunk, I didn't care who I was doing this with. He didn't have to mean a thing to me; the sound and the beat of the music had that effect on me. When I started feeling that way, I no longer made rational decisions. All that drinking and dancing with Roy gave him the wrong idea. He thought I liked him. Roy ended up taking me home and staying."

"Grandma, didn't you worry about getting VD or something back then?" Nina asked, since her health class in high school taught on sexual transmitted diseases.

"No, Child. We didn't hear about stuff like that." Before Essie Mae continued she looked at Nina and said, "As I describe Roy, always remember it's not nice to make fun of people. I'm just trying to paint a clear picture, okay Child?" Nina nodded. Essie Mae continued. "Anyway, once I let Roy spend the night, I couldn't get rid of him. He was so ugly that when I wasn't drunk, I was ashamed to be seen with him. He was short and ugly... had those big thick, red lips, a big gut, and he was very black and balding. He had a tooth missing in front. He didn't like to bathe; therefore he had a body odor that you could smell across the room."

"Oh, Grandma, he sounds horrible!" Nina said, frowning.

"There was nothing about him that appealed to me, except he didn't mind buying me booze. I'd tell him to leave, but he continued to hang around. He had a car and took me anywhere I wanted to go. He was generous, but he smelled and I just didn't like him. He would buy groceries or give me a little money and I wouldn't say anything for a while and he just kept hanging around. Like I said, when drunk, I wasn't capable of making rational decisions. If I had been in my right mind, I would never have gotten involved with him. There was a time in my life when I wouldn't have given him the time of day. So you see how low I had gotten. For booze and a little money, I let this man that made my skin crawl at his very touch when I was sober; I let him stay in my house and sleep in my bed. Valjean would tell me, 'Essie Mae, the man has got to go. He's stinking up the whole house.' I would tell him to leave, berate him about his looks and smell, but he wouldn't budge. He was like a leech that wouldn't let go. We, Valjean and I, actually nicknamed him, "The Leech."'"

"So, how did you finally get rid of him, Grandma?"

"Sadly, I'm getting to that part. You'd better put in a new tape, because I'm getting ready to tell you the best part-the worst part-and the saddest part," Essie Mae said remorsefully.

Nina looked at her grandmother and saw that her countenance had changed. "Do you want me to get you something to drink, Grandma?" she asked.

Essie Mae shook her head, indicating she did, and Nina rushed to the kitchen and brought her a glass of lemonade that Essie Mae always kept available. She took a sip of it and took a deep breath and let it out as if to say, now here goes.

"It happened one cold, wintry Friday night. It was about six o'clock. Valjean and her man were in her room watching television. The news was on because I could here it through their open door. I was in the kitchen, and Roy was in my bedroom. Earlier, Valjean had made the comment again about Roy leaving. It was cold and all the doors and windows had to be closed and there wasn't anything that could help Roy's stench. I agreed with Valjean and told her once and for all, I was getting rid of Roy.

"I was in the kitchen cutting up a chicken and thinking how I was going to tell him firmly and wasn't taking no for an answer. I had just finished cutting up the chicken and had put it in a pot of water to let it soak a little. I placed the butcher knife on the counter and was getting ready to clean out the sink when Roy walked in. Immediately I started my spill. As soon as I began to talk, Valjean closed her bedroom door, I'm assuming to give me privacy. It went something like this...

"Listen, Roy, I'm sorry, but you're going to have to find someplace else to live. You can't stay here anymore. I know we've had this conversation before and you didn't take me seriously. But I'm dead serious right now," I said, looking down into his eyes. "Valjean feels the same way I do," I continued. "This is her place too. You've been here for almost a month and I just can't take it any longer. To tell the truth, you stink up the joint! When are you going to take a bath? A bath every other week just isn't cutting it."

"I wasn't drunk when we had this conversation. I

may have had a couple of beers. Beer didn't make me drunk, it just gave me a little-what we use to call 'buzz."

"I didn't give Roy a chance to say hardly anything-I kept spewing out the insults. I didn't care if I was hurting his feelings or not. Back then I was cold hearted. I didn't notice him clenching his fists and breathing hard as he was getting more and more angry as I continued to spew out the hateful insults. I remember saying, 'You probably don't have anywhere to go. You stink so bad that nobody wants you around.' Before I knew it he had reach up and slapped me. *'You stupid wench,'* he said. *'Shut your filthy mouth'.* Both of his hands were around my neck, and he began to squeeze hard. All the while he was choking me, he was saying, *'You ungrateful wench, I give you anything you ask for. I even give you my heart, and this is how you treat me.'*

He was squeezing harder and harder, and it was getting difficult to breathe. My survival instincts kicked in and I started hitting him. But my hands didn't have any effect on him. The promise I made myself that no man would ever hurt me again flooded my mind. I reached behind me and felt the butcher knife that I had just cut the chicken up with. I wrapped my fingers around it and brought it around in front of me. Without hesitation, and with all of my strength, I plunged that butcher knife into his stomach and pulled it out. He released my throat and grabbed his stomach. He had this strange look on his face.

"Now get out,' I said. 'And I don't want to see that ugly face of yours ever again.' He turned and took a couple of steps and collapsed. I looked at the knife in my hand. It was covered with blood. I immediately turned to the sink and turned the water on to wash off the blood. The whole time I was thinking Roy was walking out the door. But when I heard him fall, I turned and looked at him. What I saw made me let out such an awful scream that Valjean and her boyfriend came running. 'What's wrong, what's wrong?" they kept asking. I pointed to the floor where Roy lay. 'Essie Mae, what have you done?!' asked Valjean.

"There lay Roy in a pool of blood. Blood was running out from under him and I couldn't think straight. I must have gone into shock or something. I kept telling Roy to get up. 'Get up, Roy. Please get up,' I kept saying. Then for some reason I thought I had to clean up that blood. I went and got several towels and tried to wipe up the blood. I smeared blood everywhere. I had never seen so much blood. Valjean kept saying, 'Call an ambulance, call an ambulance.' When the ambulance came, the police came with it. The ambulance attendant took Roy's pulse and said, *This man is dead.*' I started screaming again. I didn't want to hear those words. I stood there screaming with blood all over me. Valjean tried to comfort me while the police asked questions. Valjean's boyfriend gave what few answers he knew, and Valjean gave what little information she knew. But I alone knew what had happened, and I wasn't capable of being coherent. The ambulance attendant determined that Roy had been stabbed, and according to the information given to the police by Valjean and her boyfriend, I was the only one in the room with Roy, so the police put handcuffs on me and put me, still covered with Roy's blood, into the police car and took me to jail."

"Oh, Grandma, you killed a man?!" Nina said in a shocked whisper.

"Yeah, Baby, I did. I still can't believe I did such an awful thing," she said remorsefully. "Now you see why it has been so hard to tell you. I have not repeated this account since it happened. I buried it so deep that for years I couldn't remember it ever happened. Thank God for his forgiving grace. Only his love for me gives me the strength to share this with you now."

Essie Mae began to cry and couldn't stop. It was if the years of not remembering suddenly came forth in rivers of tears. Nina quickly went over to her and held her in her arms as she cried. Nina couldn't help but to cry along with the grandmother that she dearly loved, the grandmother whose past life sounded like a horror movie. Who would have thought a simple question like, "Grandma, how did you get those scars?" would have brought forth such awful revelations?

Nina suggested that they stop and have lunch. She was hoping something to eat would make Essie Mae feel better and that her tears would stop flowing. As she headed to the kitchen, she paused long enough to put on a gospel tape by Essie Mae's favorite singing group. The music began to soothe Essie Mae's spirit. Before long she joined Nina in the kitchen, and they sat and ate roast chicken sandwiches and some cantaloupe. Nina chatted about her friends and told some tales about what happened at college. She expressed how much she really wanted that job at the ad agency that she applied for the day before. "I hope they call soon," she said.

"Don't worry," Essie Mae said, "If it's for you, you'll get it. Just have faith." "Yes ma'am," Nina said.

"The music, the food, the conversation has done wonders for me. Are you ready to get back to the story?" Essie Mae asked after about an hour of chit chat and food. "Only if you are up to it, Grandma. I don't like to see you so upset."

"I'm okay. I needed to wash that pain out of me. It has been bottled up for nearly forty years. I feel so much better. I feel like I've just dropped a very heavy load. Come on. Let me finish my story."

They headed back to the sunroom. In the afternoon, the sun no longer shone through the window. The backyard was getting most of the sun. The room was still full of light, and the plants were healthy and green. Oh how she loved to sit in her sunroom. It never failed to bring her comfort. And it hadn't failed today. Nina could see why she felt that way about it. The coziness of the lively green plants, the brightness of the daylight that the windows allowed in, brought an air of peace about the room. This was the perfect place, if there was a perfect place, for Essie Mae to tell about this awful part of her life. The peacefulness of the room helped Essie Mae to continue.

"At the jail, they took my fingerprints and a picture. I know I looked horrible. At the time, the way I looked was the last thing on my mind. I was in a state of shock and don't remember what they asked me to do. I just went along with them. Eventually, I was put into a cell, and I sat on the bed looking at my bloody hands for hours. A female police officer came and got me and took me to a bathroom and told me to strip. I had to take off every stitch of clothing and she had to search me all over. 'Bend over and open up,' I heard her say. I couldn't believe what I was hearing. But I did it after she repeated it again with a tone that said, 'You better do it.' That was my first of many embarrassing moments. She put me under the shower and I washed all the blood off and she gave me a gray cotton dress with a white collar. The dress was two sizes to large. I didn't get a bra, but I did get a pair of panties. I was given some black slippers that were too big, so they went flip flop as I walked. When I got back to my cell, I was alert enough to see the condition of it. It smelled something awful. The bed looked dirty, and the sink and commode was stained and old. I couldn't believe I was in a place like that. My mind drifted to Mama. *What will she think of me being in a place like this?* I thought. *Maybe no one will tell her.* I hoped no one would tell her. She had warned me so many times to straighten up before something terrible happened to me. I didn't obey and there I was sitting in jail for killing a man!

CHAPTER 9

"It was a week before Val jean came to see me. She said she hadn't been allowed to visit. I could see fear in her eyes when she looked at me-fear of what was going to happen to me. My children visited me. That same fear was in their eyes. I tried to reassure them that everything would work out all right. I assured them I'd be home soon. Mama never came. I was glad. Maybe that meant she didn't know. I didn't cry out to her like I did when I was in the hospital in excruciating pain after being set on fire," Essie Mae remembered. "I was sure in a couple of months, I would be home. She didn't have to know anything about it. I told myself it was all a bad dream anyway. But I was shocked back into reality when I heard what the attorney said.

"I was assigned a court-appointed attorney. He asked me what happened. After I told him, he said he would have me plead guilty to manslaughter. I almost screamed it- 'What! Why not self-defense, Roy was choking me!

I had to defend myself. He was trying to kill me!' The attorney said since I didn't have any witnesses to Roy choking me and I didn't have any bruises to show that I had been choked, manslaughter was the best he could do for me. He said the police had charged me with first-degree murder and if found guilty, I could be put away for life or even get the gas chamber. Boy, fear gripped my heart then. I was in more trouble than I thought. All the while I was sure self-defense would get me off."

"What does manslaughter mean?" asked Nina.

"Manslaughter is killing someone without planning in advance to do it. I hadn't planned to kill Roy," Essie Mae said. "I just wanted him to leave.

"Anyway, I went to court before a judge and heard my attorney tell him my story and asked that the charges be dropped from first-degree murder to manslaughter. The judge said since I hadn't been in trouble before, he would agree to manslaughter with a sentence of three years in prison. When I heard that, I literally fainted. I woke up with the female police officer putting water on my face. *It must be a dream,* I thought. It couldn't be happening to me. I can't go to prison for three years?! But that's what the judge had said. The gavel banged loudly. There was no turning back. My fate was sealed. I was taken back to the jail cell. I stayed there for six months before I was transferred to the prison. I later learned that the time I spent in jail counted toward my sentence so I only had to serve two and a half years. That was still too long.

"Boy, what an experience being in jail," Essie Mae

continued. "There was a period there when I thought I was going insane. I was lying on the cot one day when out of the blue, I felt Roy's hand around my neck-choking me. I let out this piercing scream. It brought the guards running. 'What's wrong?" they asked. 'He's choking me. Can't you see him? Get him out of here!'

"Lady, there's no one in that cell but you. You must be having a nightmare.'

"They left me alone with my nightmare. I wanted a drink of alcohol so bad. The nightmare would go away if I just had a drink, I thought. A day or so later, I was washing my hands and the sink was full of blood. I turned and looked at the floor, there was blood everywhere. It was on my hands, my clothes, and on the cot. I started screaming again. After a while, they stopped coming to see about me when I screamed. I thought I'd die if I didn't get a drink. I'd beg, moan, and cry for a drink and nobody paid me any attention. I kept so much racket, they finally took me to a hospital. They put me in the mental ward. The police thought I was crazy. But once getting to the hospital and me begging for a drink, they quickly realized I was going through withdrawals from alcohol. I heard them say, "This woman is an alcoholic and she's experiencing withdrawals. That's why she's seeing things. She's hallucinating.' I never considered myself an alcoholic, but my reaction to not drinking proved that I was one. I stayed in the hospital for about two weeks until all the alcohol was out of my system and I stopped hallucinating. Then I was taken back to that awful jail cell. I stopped craving alcohol and I stopped hallucinating, but the bad dreams stayed with me. I hated to go to sleep.

"One terrible, terrible morning, I was awakened to a big burly female voice. 'Rise and shine ladies, we're going for a little ride.' I had no idea what she meant. There were about five of us females that never left the jail. Other women came and went. Some were in for shoplifting, prostitution, or being drunk in public. But after a few days, they were gone. How I envied them. I knew my sentence was three long years. Sometimes I would cry myself to sleep. How did I get here? I asked myself, I bet, a thousand times." Essie Mae said.

"The five of us got dressed, not only in our clothes, but handcuffs as well. We were cuffed to each other. One by one we stepped up on an old rickety bus that had 'State of North Carolina Prison System' written on the side of it. Anyone who saw that bus would know we were what they called convicts convicted of a serious crime. Me-Essie Mae Billings Bedford, a convict at age fifty-seven. I just couldn't believe it. I was as scared as I could be sitting on that bus heading to Raleigh-to the state prison for Women. I learned where we were going from listening to the other women talk. One of them had been there before. She violated her parole and now she was headed back. She tried to make it sound like no big deal. But she wasn't as brave as she wanted us to think she was.

"Don't worry, girls, it's not that bad,' she said, laughing. 'You just have to watch your back.'

"What did she mean by that? I wondered. Fear gripped me even tighter.

"The ride was long and bumpy on that rickety old bus. We stopped once to use the rest room and to get something to eat. I was so embarrassed when people looked at us. Even though I didn't know them, I couldn't look anyone in the face I was so ashamed of myself. There was an officer with a shotgun and a gun on his hip watching us the entire time.

"All the while the bus rumbled down the highway, all of us sat very quietly-staring out the window, dealing with our own thoughts. Mine was filled with prayers. I never prayed so much in my life. When I thought of three years in prison, I'd pray, 'Dear Lord, how am I going to make it? You are going to have to help me,' I pleaded. I thought of Mama. I knew she prayed for me a lot. I was hoping she hadn't stopped because I needed her prayers more than ever.

"Suddenly, the girl who had been to prison before broke the silence.

"Hey,' she said. "I'm Lucy. What's ya'll's name?' She looked questioningly at each of us. The first girl said, 'Frances. The next said, 'Florene.' When it came to me, I managed to whisper, 'Essie Mae' and the next girl said her name was Maggie. Lucy didn't leave it at just knowing our names; she wanted to know what we were in for. I was not in the mood for conversation. I was too gripped with fear. I don't think the others wanted to talk either, but they were afraid not to. Frances and Florene said what they were in for, but I don't remember what they said. When it was my turn, I kept my head down and didn't say anything. Lucy said, 'Essie Mae, what's your crime?' I burst out crying and cried for about five minutes. By the time I'd stopped crying and had wiped away my tears and snot on my dress tail, Lucy had lost interest and I was glad. She tried to be consoling. She said, 'Look, it's not that bad. Just don't go in acting like a wimp or a scaredy cat. They will have you doing whatever they want you to do. Go in acting like you're brave even if you are scared to death.'

"Looming ahead was a huge brick building surrounded by a fence of barbed wire-sharp as razors. Lucy yelled, 'Look ahead, girls, there's your new home.' My heart began to race faster, and my stomach knotted tighter. I felt like I was going to throw up at any second. My legs were like rubber when it was time to get off the bus. The girl in front of me sort of pulled me along, and the one behind me sort of pushed me on. I managed to get off the bus. We were taken to a processing room. The two guards handed over some papers and signed us over and walked out without taking a second look at us. I wanted to run after them and beg them to take me back, I didn't belong there. I sat as stiff as a board on that hard bench until someone called my name.

"We lined up to get our prison gear, which consisted of a small bag of toiletries-toothbrush, toothpaste, a bar of soap, and some deodorant. Then we got a towel, a loose- fitting dress, and some underwear. We were led down a narrow hall to a large community bathroom where we were told to strip off all our clothes. There they gave us another degrading search of our bodies. We were told to take a shower and put on the prison clothes. After we were dressed, we were taken to our cells. We were not put together. We were put in with strangers. It would have been nice to have been put in the same cell. Even though we didn't know one another, we had at least shared a few hours together on the bus.

"My first night in prison was spent staring at the ceiling. I don't think I slept at all. I was put in a cell with three other women. There were two bunk beds. My bed was a top bunk. I tried not to move much, in fear of disturbing the girl below me. I could hear other women yelling, 'Shut the f-k up' to someone who was talking in a soft tone. Boy, the language they used there! I use to say a few cuss words before, but nothing like that. But while there, I had to use the same vulgar language they used to make me seem like one of the crowd. Thank God, when he saved me, he washed all that filthiness out of me," Essie Mae bragged.

"I was there a month and it felt like a year. I thanked God for letting me make it there a month. I was so bored. We were assigned duties. I got assigned to the laundry room. I didn't mind that much, at least I was busy. For recreation they offered needlepoint, macrame, sewing classes, and ceramic. I tried to take advantage of all of them to keep busy. I had very few visitors. I wrote to Valjean and begged her to come see me. But it was hard since her boyfriend's car wasn't very reliable. My children came now and then. I understood it was a long trip, so I didn't blame them. Saturdays and Sundays were the hardest days. Those were the days for visitors. If you didn't have a visitor, you stayed in your cell. I spent most of my Saturdays and Sundays in my cell. Sunday morning they'd let you go to church service if you wanted to. I went, but the person directing the service acted like he didn't know who he was supposed to be teaching about. One good thing I got from there was a Bible. They had a table full of them with a sign that said, 'Free, take one.' I gladly took one and it became my best friend. Now my Saturdays and Sundays were spent lying in my bunk reading my Bible. I began at Genesis and read all the way through to Revelation. I did this about three or four times before I was released," Essie Mae recalled.

"I bet it was hard living in a cell with three other women and a commode, wasn't it Grandma?" Nina asked.

"Child, let me tell you," Essie Mae groaned. It's something I wouldn't wish on anyone. Boy, the whole prison smelled bad, but in the cell it actually stunk. Passing gas, smelly body odor, and stinking breath was very hard to take. But when you don't have a choice, you get used to anything. As time went by, I began to cope. I was still fearful and I never felt relaxed, but I had gotten into the routine of prison life. I was getting to know Jesus from reading the Bible every chance I got. I was beginning to understand what Mama was saying and why she wanted all her children to get saved. I read how Jesus loved me so that he died for me. And If I asked him to come into my heart, he would come in and he would never leave me nor forsake me. Silently one night as I lay on my bunk, amid the snoring and passing gas of my cellmates, I asked him to come into my heart and I believed he did. I felt a little different. Even though I was still scared to be in prison, something inside felt different," Essie Mae remembered.

CHAPTER 10

"Days slowly went by. I had been there about a year when I took up sewing and ceramic. The sewing group kind of hung together when we went on the yard for recreation. We rarely talked. We just sat up in the stands and watched the others below. It was so good to be out in the fresh air and sunshine. One day out of the blue, I heard someone call my name. I was startled. It was Lucy, the girl that was on the bus that brought us to prison. I hadn't seen her since that day.

"Hey, Essie Mae. You still scared?' she said in a loud voice so that several heads turned to look in the direction she was looking.

"I couldn't believe she was singling me out. I hung my head and hoped no one knew she was referring to me. What made it worse, the four 'go for bad' women in the prison that everyone tried to avoid, heard her. They were trouble makers and carried knives, so it was said. They were walking by as Lucy was making fun of me. Then Lucy did a very terrible thing. She pointed at me and said to those bad girls, 'You see Essie Mae up there on them steps. She's a scaredy cat. I rode with her on the bus and she cried all the way here.' The girls looked my way and made vulgar gestures that made me cringe. I pretended she wasn't talking to me and hoped those girls didn't realize it was me Lucy was talking about. I had tried to keep a very low profile, biding my time until I could get out. Now Lucy had made me a target. I never knew why she did that unless to shift the focus off her. Was this what she called 'watching your back'? She pretends to be their friend by giving them someone to bully. That way, they wouldn't bother her. There I was probably the most timid woman in prison now the target for the meanest women in prison. Oh, God, help me I prayed.

"It wasn't long before those bad women had me cornered! Boy, oh boy, I've never been so scared in all my life!" Essie Mae said, throwing up her hands and bring them down to her lap to emphasize how frightened she was.

At that moment, Essie Mae's phone began to ring. Not only that, there wasa knock on the door as well. Both Essie Mae and Nina were reluctant to move. The best part of the story was about to be told. But the phone kept ringing and the person kept knocking.

"I'll get the door, Grandma, while you get the phone," Nina said and ran to the door. She saw two little girl scouts standing smiling. "Would you like to buy some cookies?" Nina hated to turn them away without buying something, but she didn't have any money. So she went to see if Essie Mae would give her some.

She heard Essie Mae saying, "I'm here entertaining my granddaughter. Yes, it is nice of her to spend her summer days with her old grandmother. Nina is just nice that way. Martha, let me call you back about that Auxiliary money- making idea. Nina and I were in the middle of something. I'll call you after supper tonight. All right. All right. Good- bye." Essie Mae hung up the phone remarking, "Martha is a sweetheart, but it's hard to get her off the phone."

After promising to call Martha back and after buying a couple of boxes of Girl Scout cookies, they were ready to get back to the story but not before they had tasted the cookies and had a cold glass of milk along with them.

"Anyway I was plenty scared," Essie Mae continued. "There were five of them. All were husky and masculine looking. The leader wore her hair cut like a man and wore pants like a man. She weighed about two hundred pounds. But it wasn't fat, she was tall and big like your cousin Effie. Her eyes were hard and cold, her lips were thick, and her skin was black as soot. She looked mean. The others followed her everywhere she went. They did whatever she told them to do. They called her 'Boss.' When they walked into the cafeteria at mealtime, women in line would move and let them in front without protest. Wherever they went, they had fearful respect from all the prisoners. Sometimes the guards hesitated to cross them. Someone said once a prisoner bumped into her and didn't say 'excuse me' or anything. The next day they found her dead. She had been beaten and stabbed. Everyone believed those mean women did it. Nothing was done about it since they couldn't prove it. Now here I am cornered by these same brutal women.

"A couple of weeks after I was singled out, I was doing my job in the laundry room as I normally did each day. Some days the same women would have the same shift I did. There would be a group assigned to sort the clothes, a group to keep the washing machines and dryers going, and a group to fold the clothes that were dry. I was in the folding group. We'd fold clothes until our shoulders ached. One woman loved to talk about her family. We'd fold clothes and listen to her talk until our shift was over. On this particular day when I entered the laundry room, I noticed I didn't see any of the usual girls. The group I was folding with was all strangers. I figured the others had gotten reassigned. Things changed often, and we were never given explanations. We just did what we were told and didn't ask questions.

"I grabbed an armful of clothes and started folding. I had a couple of piles of dresses folded neatly on the table and had reached for another armful when I heard the double doors bang open. In walked those mean women, and they were headed my direction."

"Grandma, what did you do? How did you get away alive?" asked Nina.

"I'm about to tell you. Do you remember you asked me if I believed in angels? Well what I'm about to tell you will prove to you that I most definitely believe in angels.

"As I said, the double doors banged open. The girls that were folding with me disappeared quickly. I glanced around to see if there was anyone that I could call to help me. There was no one in sight. No one at the washing machines and dryers, no one at the sorting bins. Everyone had disappeared but me. The women had smirks on their faces as they approached me. My heart started pounding, and my breathing must have nearly stopped, because it felt like I wasn't getting enough air.

"Hey, b--ch, you scared?' the boss asked, looking at me and grinning.

"I hated her calling me that word. I hate to use it now, but I feel I must be as actual as possible since you have to write this story. But don't you ever talk like that, you hear?" Essie Mae never missed a chance to let Nina know that vulgar talk would never be tolerated by her.

"I was so scared, I couldn't speak if I wanted to," Essie Mae went on.

"Take her, girls,' the boss ordered her followers.

"One took my right arm, one took my left arm, one took my right leg, and the other one took my left leg. They lifted me up on the table. I started to scream then. They slapped me and said, 'Shut up. We're not going to hurt you-not much anyway. We're here to have a little fun. Just relax and maybe you'll enjoy it.' Boy, I began to pray then. 'Oh Lord, please, please help me. Help me Jesus, I pleaded. They roared with laughter and mocked me and said, 'Let's see if Jesus going to help her. Even if he did exist, he wouldn't be nowhere near you in this place. But if it makes you feel any better, keep on calling him.' I called him with all my might. Jesus you said to call on you in time of trouble. You said you would never leave me nor forsake me. I tried to remember what I had been reading in the Bible.

"The boss said, "Tear off her clothes. One of them grabbed the front of my dress and yanked it and it ripped, exposing my bra. Then I felt a hand on my thigh moving up toward my panties and I did cry out to Jesus even harder then. 'Jesus, you said call unto you and you would answer. Help now Lord!'

"Put a sock in her mouth and shut her up,' the boss said. 'I don't want to hear anymore of that Jesus stuff?

"One of them jammed a sock in my mouth. I kept on screaming and praying, even though it came out muffled. Just in the nick of time, I heard a voice say with such authority like I've never heard before Leave her alone!'

"And who's going to make us?' the boss said, moving toward this large woman who was about the size of the boss herself.

I said "Leave her alone!" the woman repeated.

"The boss motioned to her girls, who finally loosened their grip on me and whipped out their makeshift knives. Two of the girls went over and grabbed my rescuer by the arms. She lifted her arms up, and the two women went flying across the room like rag dolls. The boss motioned to the other two girls, and they approached the woman with knives. She grabbed each hand and squeezed it until they were whimpering like little puppies. The boss looked scared then and didn't try to do anything herself. She gathered up her group, and they went limping out of the room. The stranger had done all that without much effort. She was like Wonder Woman. After the boss and her crew left, the stranger looked at me cowering on the table trying to cover my body and said, 'Jesus does hear prayers even in a place like this.' She turned and left. She has never spoken another word to me."

"Wow, Grandma, that's awesome!" Nina interrupted.

"Even though I never heard her voice again," Essie Mae continued, "I did see her again. It was she who helped me get through the next year and a half. Whenever I felt danger, I'd look around and she would be standing somewhere nearby. The boss and her cronies didn't like being beaten. So they wanted to kill her and me. But they could never get near me without first seeing her. They were afraid to get too close to her. They tried to find out about her, but no one could tell them anything. The boss approached different guards about her, but they told her she was seeing things. There wasn't anyone like that in that prison. Even when they pointed her out to them, they couldn't see her. I truly believe she was an angel sent to help me. No one could see her but me and those mean women. I never saw her talking to anyone. I only saw her when I was afraid. I'd look around and she'd be standing with her arm folded. Her complexion was as smooth as a baby's and it seemed to glow. Her hair was shiny black and was always styled so beautifully-not a strand out of place. Her eyes were full of compassion, and when I'd look into them, all my fear would melt away.

"Yes, she was my angel. I haven't seen her since then. I haven't been in great distress since then. I believe she'd come if I needed her."

"Grandma, I believe she did come back. Remember when you had that mild heart attack a couple of years ago?"

"Yeah, I remember. The Good Lord saw fit to leave me here I believe to tell you this story." "Anyway, the night you got sick, I was asleep. I thought I was dreaming. I heard someone calling me, 'Nina, Nina wake up!' I wanted to wake up but I couldn't. Then I felt someone hit me on my thigh, right here," Nina said, pointing. "I woke up with a stinging sensation right here on my thigh. Then I had the urge to go in and check on you and found you gasping for air. I believe your angel woke me that night, Grandma," said Nina.

"It could have been, honey. I do believe our God watches over us. So many people don't believe. But I want you to write this story and maybe someone will read it and believe in the power of Jesus. He's an awesome God!"

"Grandma, it is so hard to believe all these things happened to you. What a life you have lived. I wouldn't want to go through half the stuff you've been through. But look at you now. You are loving, kind, and always giving to other people. Grandma, when you got out of prison, what did you do? Where did you live?"

"Well, when it was time for me to get out, I wondered what I'd do or where I'd go. It had been three years, and Valjean had gotten someone else to move in to help with the rent. I didn't want to be a burden on my children. But your mother begged me to come live with her. You were four years old. You and I had a lot of fun together."

"Yeah, I remember," Nina said.

"I stayed with you all for about a year until I found a job living with a family where I took care of the house, cooking and cleaning. That's how I got this house, you know."

"No, Grandma, tell me about that."

"That's not as dramatic like my other stories, but it is a story about God's goodness. I tell you, that first year I was out of prison was rough. I stayed inside most of the time. Wherever I went, I felt like everyone was looking at me funny. I could almost hear them snickering, saying, 'She's a jailbird.' Of course, that was all in my mind. Everyone was friendly toward me. But it was me who felt ashamed, and I hadn't forgiven myself for what I did to put me in prison. I even had some nightmares about prison. The dreams were mostly about those mean women coming after me. I'd wake up in a cold sweat; thanking God it was a dream. If I wasn't dreaming about those women, I'd dream about being locked in a cage and couldn't get out. I would be struggling and screaming let me out! Please let me out! I'd wake up tangled up in the covers. It would take me all day to get over a dream like that."

"I think I remember that. I would want to play with

you, and Mama would say, 'Don't bother Grandma today. She's not feeling well," Nina recalled.

"I'm glad your mother was a church-goer. It was at church that I was set free of that bondage." "Is this when you got converted and became a Christian?" Nina asked.

"Yes. This is when I got reborn. This is when my old life was wiped away and my new life began. How good it is to tell you some good news for a change.

"I remember it was revival time. There was a lot of singing, clapping hands, and shouting. I clapped my hands too since everyone was clapping, but I didn't feel like doing it. Then there were some, men and women, who were actually shouting, jumping around, and hollering, *Thank you, Jesus. I love you, Jesus.*" I wondered how in the world they could make such a spectacle of themselves. I said to myself I would never do that. I didn't think about how I used to act in the nightclubs, bumping and grinding with men; with men I didn't even know half the time. But then, I was having fun, or so I thought.

"The minister began to preach. He seemed to be directing his sermon straight at me. He said, 'Some of you sitting in here are ashamed to praise the Lord. You know He's been good to you. The Bible says in the Book of Psalms, 'Make a joyful noise unto the Lord. Shout with gladness. Sing high praises unto him. Praise him for his mighty acts: praise him according to his excellent greatness'. Praise ye the Lord. Sing unto the Lord a new song, and his praise in the congregation of saints. Let them praise his name in the dance; Let them sing praises unto him with the timbrel and harp. Psalm

146:7 says he gives food to the hungry. The Lord looseth the prisoners. Can anyone in here say amen to that?"

"I wanted to know how he knew I had been a prisoner. I wondered if your mother had talked to him. He went on, 'How many of you have called on the Lord and he answered your call? When you were in trouble, he was there. When you needed food, he was there. When you needed someplace to stay, he made a way for you, didn't he? Why be ashamed of him now? You need to repent of your sinful ways. Do you need to get closer to God tonight? Don't you want Jesus to live in your heart? Come to the altar right now and ask for forgiveness and accept Jesus as your savior. Serve him with all your heart and you'll never regret it. And when Jesus comes into your heart, you will receive the Holy Spirit and he will be your comforter. Do you need a comforter tonight? Don't go home without him. He loves you so much. Didn't he prove his love for you when you were desperate and you called on him, didn't he show up?'

"Suddenly I could see myself lying helpless on that table with those women holding me down and me screaming for Jesus to help me and in walks God's angel and saved me. I couldn't sit still any longer. Uncontrollable tears started flowing from my eyes. I jumped up and I pushed my way out into the aisle-stepping on toes as I did and rushed to the altar crying, 'Lord Jesus forgive me. Please forgive me for all the awful sins I've committed. Come into my heart and make me a new person.' I don't know how long I knelt at that altar crying. It was about five or six of us there. The minister asked us to stand to our feet and repeat the sinner's prayer. After we finished praying, he laid hands on each of us individually and said, 'You are now a new creation in Christ. Receive the Holy Ghost.' Some stood, some fell. But when he got to me and placed his hand on my forehead and said, 'You are now a new creation in Christ. Receive the Holy Ghost,' I started trembling and I felt a heat on my head and it traveled down my body until it touched my feet. When it touched my feet, I started jumping ... just like the people earlier. I couldn't help myself. I had this joy inside that I couldn't control. It made me feel like screaming, jumping, running it was such a wonderful feeling. I had said sarcastically earlier that it didn't take all that. But I didn't know any better. Until someone experiences what the Lord allowed me to experience, they should never determine what it takes to worship our Lord. I praised the Lord all the way home, into the night and the next day. Ever since then, me and the Lord have been very close. He talks to me in his Word, in my spirit, and through praise. It is a wonderful thing to be filled with the Holy Ghost.

"I wanted to share this new experience with everyone I came in contact with. I was no longer embarrassed about once being in prison. I was a new creation-old things had passed away, all things had become new. I became a new woman at the age of sixty-one. I felt happy and full of joy. Before I didn't feel like doing anything or going anywhere, but after that night, I had more energy than I knew what to do with. The first person I decided to share this new joy with was my best friend,

Valjean. She had been coming around asking me to go out with her. She wanted me to pick up where I'd left off. But I turned her down. I didn't want to go back to that old life. I didn't want to drink anymore. Valjean wanted to introduce me to something that was better than whiskey, she said. She had some pills she wanted me to try.

"Come on, girl, try a pill. You will get a high like no other. My new roommate's boyfriend can get all you want. He sells them,' Valjean said.

"I looked at her, and I knew she was going in a dangerous direction. I'd heard women in prison talking about taking pills. Some were in there for taking them and for selling them. Drugs were the new thing of the day and I didn't want any part of it.

"Come on, Essie Mae, this isn't like you,' Valjean said to me with a bewildered expression on her face. "You used to be the life of the party. What happened to you in prison? Everyone knows you're home and they have been waiting for you to come back and join the group.'

"I'm sorry, Valjean," I said, "but I just don't have a desire to return to that scene.'

"Valjean wasn't taking no for an answer. She threw her trump card out.

"Essie Mae, I got this fine-looking man I want you to meet. I've told him about you and he wants to meet you. I know you must be ready to meet a man after being shut way for three years,' Valjean said with a wink.

"Does he take pills too?"

"Of course. Everyone that we hang with takes them.'

"Look, Valjean, I love you like my own sister. But this drug thing isn't for me. It shouldn't be for you either. Girl, that stuff is dangerous. It can land you in prison too. I saw several women who were in there for drugs. Valjean, I beg you to leave that mess alone.'

"I love you too. But this is my life and I'm going to live it. I'm not going to sit around like you have been doing for the last year. I'll see you around, Essie Mae,' Valjean said and walked out.

"She stopped coming to see me. But after my conversion, I had this great desire to find her and tell her about this wonderful thing that I had. Something that was much better than drugs!"

"Was it hard to get her to believe what you were saying?" Nina asked.

"Baby, you just don't know. I felt like giving up several times, but I cared too much for her to let her die and go to hell. At first when I started visiting her, she was glad because she thought I had finally decided to start hanging out with her again. But after a while, she hated to see me come around. 'All you talk about is Jesus this and Jesus that. Frankly, I'm tired of hearing it,' she told me one day. I'd knock on her door and she would pretend she wasn't home. Or if she opened the door, she'd be so high that she'd make fun of everything I said. 'Come on in, preacher woman, and let me hear some more of that Jesus talk,' she'd say. I'd tell her that I loved her and Jesus loved her too each time before I walked out of her house. At least she'd heard it. It took me a year and a half of doing that before she finally accepted Jesus as her Lord and Savior."

"What made her finally give in, Grandma?" Nina asked.

"She almost died. She was taking all kinds of drugs and drinking too. Every new drug that came along, she would try it. Finally, she tried something new while she was already drinking and she overdosed. Someone called and told me she was in the hospital dying. I rushed over to see her. When I walked into that hospital room, I could hardly believe my eyes. The person I saw didn't look like Valjean at all. She was black as night, and if she weighed ninety pounds, I would be exaggerating. Her hair was matted to her head as if it hadn't been combed in weeks. The skin on her face was drawn tight, and she looked like an old woman of ninety. My heart broke for her. *How did it come to this?* I wondered. I remembered how beautiful and sexy the two of us thought we were when we were young. We both had shapes that caused men to flock to us. *Now look at us,* I thought. *I'm full of scars,* and she has wasted to nothing. Scars or no, I told myself, I had something that Valjean needed and I wasn't going to give up trying to give it to her. I moved close to her bed and began calling her name softly.

"Valjean, Valjean. It's me Essie Mae. Can you hear me?'

"She didn't respond. She had a tube in her arm and in her nose. She was barely breathing. I held her hand and began to pray softly. I read Scripture out loud so she could hear me. I wanted God's word to go into her conscious and subconscious mind. In a week's time, I read the whole book of Psalms and she didn't stir once. But I was determined not to give up. I didn't want my best friend's soul to be lost. She was already in hell, in my opinion. She needed something better. I stayed by her side until visiting hours were over. I'd whisper, 'Valjean, I have to leave now, but I'll be back tomorrow.' I took a small bottle of oil from my purse, and placed some on the tip of my finger and placed it on her forehead and prayed and asked God to spare her life, before I left the room.

"The following day I when back to visit her. I walked into the room and looked at Valjean. She still had the tubes in her arm, but the one that had been in her nose was gone. She appeared to be asleep. I said, 'Valjean, Valjean, this is Essie Mae, can you hear me. Valjean, Valjean?' I kept calling her. Valjean finally said, 'Yeah. I can hear your loud mouth, Essie Mae, stop calling my name!" I knew Valjean was on the mend. She was talking like her old self. I praised the Lord. He had answered my prayer. I sat with Valjean all that day and told her about the goodness of the Lord. Just before I had to leave, I asked her, 'Valjean, won't you accept Jesus as your Lord and Savior? Do you know what she said? She said, 'Yeah, I'll do it. If I don't you're going to worry me to death, aren't you?' I said, 'Yeah. I sure am.' She prayed the sinner's prayer after me.

"On the way home, I began to think I was like the woman in Luke 18, the one who continued to go to the judge, begging him for justice. She would not quit even although the judge kept sending her away. Because of her persistence, he gave her what she asked for. I thought, because of my persistence, Val jean would not die and go to hell. I felt good."

"Did she say yes just to make you leave her alone? What happened after she got out of the hospital?" Nina inquired.

"You don't think I'd let her get off that easy, do you? I continued to visit her and talked more about the Bible. By the time Valjean was strong and healthy again, she was ready to start going to church on a regular basis. She got filled with the Holy Ghost and faithfully served the Lord for the rest of her life. She actually found a saved man and they got married and they started a church in another state. Before she moved, she and I were two best friends sharing the same interest again. We showed as much zeal about the things of the Lord as we did when we were having fun with the devil. She and I did some wonderful things for the Lord before she met 'the Reverend,' as she called him, and moved away. I sure did miss her. But I was happy she finally found someone to love her; and they both loved the Lord. Their love was like Jocko's and mine. I was happy, they had a good marriage. Valjean finally found what she had been looking for all along. She'll always be my best friend. I sure enjoyed seeing her when she showed up for my special day you gave me a couple of years ago. Remember?"

"I sure do, Grandma. Grandma, I wonder why the

Lord didn't send someone to love you once you got saved like he did for Valjean. You deserve to be loved, too."

"I don't know, Child. I never questioned him about that. I'm just so happy to be where I am. I have no reason to complain."

"Grandma, you haven't told me how you got this house," Nina said, trying to get her to keep talking, for she was truly enjoying hearing the story of the most interesting person she had come across in her young life. She didn't think she could sit that long and listen to anyone else.

"Ah, this house!" she said with joy. This house was truly a blessing from God. I'll tell you about that after lunch. Come on, let's see what we can find in the kitchen," Essie Mae said, rising slowly from her chair. Her joints had gotten stiff from sitting so long.

It was around 2:30 in the afternoon before they returned to the porch to pick up where they'd left off.

"Let's see," Essie Mae started, "I had been staying with you all for over a year. I couldn't find work. I'd go on interviews and as soon as I tell them what I'd been doing for the past few years, suddenly the job was not available. So I spent most of my time reading the Word, keeping the house clean, and cooking for you all-which I didn't mind at all. One day one of the saints in the church asked me if I needed a job. She said she had been offered a job, but she already had one and wasn't interested in quitting. She was asked if she knew of anyone she could recommend.

"Oh, Bertha, I would love a job,' I told her. But

you know my background. Who will hire me?" was my response.

"Essie Mae Bedford ...' she said, and I knew a good scolding was on the way.

"How can you talk like that and knowing you are a child of God? What did the Bible say you became when you got saved?'

"That I was a new creation,' I answered.

"And ...' she waited.

"Old things are passed away, behold all things have become new,' I said, reciting 2 Corinthians 5:17.

"Okay then. If you want that job, act like it. Come on, I'll take you to meet the family.'

"What will I be doing?'

"It's a housekeeping job. There are three children. The mother is frail and sickly, and they need someone to care for the house and children. I think it's a live-in job. You don't mind, do you? I thought of you right away because I knew you were living with your daughter. Also, you love the Lord and the family is looking for a Christian housekeeper because they are Christians too. Do you still want the job?' Bertha asked, watching my face to see if I had confidence in my eyes or if I was still feeling defeated.

"I want it," I said in a positive tone.

"Okay, let's go.'

"We went to meet the family. I stood just inside the door, right over there." Nina looked in the direction she pointed. "Little did I know that Bertha had already told them about my past. Also little did I know that Bertha had told them how on fire I was for the Lord and that when I prayed, things usually happened.

"Why did you tell them that, Bertha? I don't like to have people expecting great things from me when I have no power of my own,' I told Bertha on the way home.

"You got the job didn't you? Aren't you excited?'

"I was indeed excited. I was shown the small room that would be mine. In the room was a bed, nightstand with a lamp, a dresser, and a closet. The bedspread and curtains matched. It was a cheerful room. I liked it. Mr. and Mrs. Wilson were very nice. Ms. Phyllis (that's what I called her) was pale and spoke softly. But our spirits connected right away. Mr. Sam was proper and business-like. He didn't make me nervous, but I could tell he didn't go for any nonsense. I moved in the following week. I missed you all very much. But I was able to visit you on Saturdays and Sundays, remember that?"

Nina nodded.

"The Wilsons and I hit it off right from the start. The children, a boy-Samuel Jr.-everybody called him Sammy-and a girl-Cynthia, and we called her Cindy-were well mannered and we grew very close. They'd come to me for advice as they got older-introduced me to their friends and treated me with great respect. Cindy was a pretty little thing and she had lots of friends. When Sammy got to be a teenager, the girls started calling. He was a handsome boy played football and was very popular. When he and Cindy left for college-a year apart-the house became empty and quiet. But when they came home for the holidays, the house came alive again.

You could see the joy in Mr. Sam's and Ms. Phyllis' face when those two children were around. Years passed and they each graduated college and eventually got married and didn't come around that often. Mr. Sam took sick right after Cindy gave them their first grandchild. He passed away soon after. That left Ms. Phyllis all alone. I hardly had any work to do in the house; I was just there for companionship for her. She lived for the days when the grandbabies came for a visit. She'd love on them and spoil them until they didn't want to go home. They'd cry to stay at grandma's house. She bought them anything they wanted."

"Like you did me, huh, Grandma," Nina said, smiling.

"Yeah, just like I did you. I loved every minute of it, and so did she. But in between those grandbabies' visits, all she had was me.

"She often said, 'Essie Mae, I don't know what I'd do without you. One day I'm going to show you how much I appreciate you.' That day came when she died. In her will she had left me this house. I could live in it as long as I lived, all the utilities would be taken care of, any repairs would be taken care of, and I could do what I wanted to with it except sell it. So when I die, the house goes back to their estate. Cynthia and Sam Jr. will probably sell it since they have their own fabulous homes and have no need of this one. They didn't oppose their mother's decision, and if I needed anything today, all I would have to do is call one of them and they would take care of it. Now, isn't God good? I don't have to depend on my grandchildren to take care of me since I've outlived all my children. Do you know if I got to the point where I couldn't take care of myself, they would hire someone to come in and care for me?"

"Wow, Grandma, they really did love you," Nina said in awe.

"Yes, Child. Those were some of my happier days working for the Wilsons. We prayed a lot together-about jobs, about grades, boyfriends and girlfriends, sicknesses and accidents. When something went wrong, they'd find me and say, 'Essie Mae, it's time to pray!'

"It was a sad night when Ms. Phyllis drew her last breath," Essie Mae said, seeming to still feel the pain. "I sat and held her hand a long time. She knew her time was short, but she wasn't fearful. We talked about heaven and what she was going to do when she first got there. She wanted to see Jesus first of all. She said she would tell him that I was doing a good job for him on earth. She actually had a smile on her face when she died-one deep breath and that was it. Her hand went limp and I laid it gently across her chest, kissed her forehead and said, 'Goodbye, Ms. Phyllis, I'll see you later.'

"I felt so sorry for the family. They took it hard, especially the grandchildren. They missed their grandmother terribly. Sam Jr. took care of his mother's business. He was the one that told me what Ms. Phyllis had done-giving me this house and all. He told me to enjoy it and if I ever needed anything I was to call him. I rarely bother him. I did call him the day the air conditioner went out and we had to sit on the porch in the heat for a day, remember?" she asked Nina. Nina smiled and nodded her head.

Essie Mae continued on, "I didn't want to stay in this house after the funeral. I wasn't scared to; I just hated all the silence. That's when I came to live with you all for a spell, remember?"

"I remember, Grandma. Just when we got used to you being with us again, you moved back here."

"And I've been here ever since. It's been eight years now. I still put flowers on her grave on her birthday. Mine are usually less beautiful than the ones the children have placed there. But I'm sure she appreciates mine just as much."

Essie Mae had grown weary of talking and slowly got up from her chair. "Now, Child, we have talked all day," Essie Mae said to Nina. "It's time to cook supper." She put her arm around Nina's small waist and Nina placed hers around her Grandmother's waist and they walked to the kitchen together. "Tomorrow you go home and visit your family and spend some time with your friends. I don't want you to spend your whole summer with me and miss out having some fun, you hear?"

"Okay, Grandma. Maybe I'll get a call about that part-time job at the ad company tomorrow and I can go to work. Do you think it will happen, Grandma?

"Yeah, Baby, I have a good feeling about it," Essie Mae said while giving her a squeeze and a reassuring smile. Nina just knew she had that summer job!

After supper, Essie Mae headed toward her bedroom feeling relieved in spirit, yet her body felt tired. The song "Love Lifted Me" returned to her mind, and she hummed as she prepared for bed. She was glad to have told her story; now she could get back to living until the Lord called her. She felt she was ready. But in the meantime she must get busy working with the Auxiliary Club to raise money for Reverend Syke's operation. She dozed off thinking of money-making ideas.

CHAPTER 11

The summer months seemed to have flown Nina was back in college, Thanksgiving was over, and Christmas was on everybody's mind, including Essie Mae's. It was time to decorate for Christmas. She always loved a lot of lights on the porch, in the bushes, and around her windows. Her neighbors always complimented her on her beautiful decorations. Although her display prompted the other neighbors to decorate more each holiday season, Essie Mae was proud to say that hers always surpassed her neighbors. Each year right after Thanksgiving she went into the back room the room that used to be hers when she worked for the Wilsons and pulled out the huge box of lights she had neatly tucked away the year before. Her grandchildren fussed at her for dragging that heavy box out each year instead of calling one of them to help her. But Essie Mae had always been independent and liked doing for herself. She didn't like bothering anyone. Her mind told her she could do just about anything she wanted to do. But her eighty eight-year-old body didn't agree. The pain of arthritis reminded her often that she couldn't move about as swiftly as she once could. But she'd take her medicine, and when the pain was gone, she was back doing what she had been trying to do before. No amount of scolding from her granddaughter, or from Nina or from the rest of the family, could change her mind about doing what she wanted to do. That day was no different. But this time the pain she felt in her chest while pulling the heavy box of Christmas decorations into the living room was more than she could take a pill for. Essie Mae grabbed her chest while nearly collapsing to the floor. She could barely breathe. She knew she needed help. This pain was not going to go away by just sitting down and resting a spell. She struggled to move her feet that would carry her to the phone just a short distance away. But her feet felt like a ball and chain were bound to her ankle. She struggled and managed to reach the phone and dialed her granddaughter's number.

"Hello."

"The pain, the pain," she said, barely above a whisper.

"Who is this? Is that you, Grandma?" Naomi asked.

"Help me," Essie Mae said and collapsed and the phone slid from her hand.

Naomi immediately called the ambulance and told them to meet her at her grandmother's house.

Essie Mae lay there wondering if she was dying.

With the pain being so severe and not being able to breathe, she resolved herself to the fact that this was her end. She made peace with the Lord, asking him to forgive her of any sin she had not repented for. She then stopped fighting and gave in to the pain and slowly slipped into darkness; on her way to heaven, she was sure.

The ambulance and her granddaughter arrived at Essie Mae's at the same time. Rushing in, they found her collapsed on the living room floor. They felt for a pulse. There was one, a slight one, but a pulse was there. The ambulance rushed her to the emergency room. The doctors immediately started to care for her. The doctors said it didn't look good. Naomi called her husband and other family members but decided not to call Nina since she had a very important exam to study for and take that week. They didn't want anything to disrupt her studies. After several hours of waiting, the doctors came out and told them that Essie Mae was stable and they could go in and see her.

Essie Mae could hear voices before she was fully conscious. The voices she heard were familiar. They sounded like Naomi and Jim. But that couldn't be so. They were not in heaven. She opened her eyes to see a nurse handling some tubes and a doctor talking to her granddaughter Naomi. "This isn't heaven," she said.

"No, Grandmama, you're in the hospital. You are still alive," Naomi said, gently stroking her hand.

"I expected to wake up in Jesus' arms hearing the

heavenly angels sing. Why did you have to mess things up?"

The doctors said it was the medication that was making her talk like that. But Essie Mae knew it was no medication. She was disappointed to wake up still alive, even more so when the doctors began to tell her all the things she wouldn't be able to do. She would not be able to live alone again. She'd have to have someone to look after her around the clock. All the foods she loved, she couldn't eat anymore. Essie Mae never wanted to be a burden to anyone. Now just look at me, she thought – *helpless*. Who is going to look after me? Why would the Lord bring me back to be a burden on my children? All kinds of thoughts were running through Essie Mae's mind. Soon her thoughts started running together and she drifted off to sleep.

The next morning the nurse came in cheerfully with her breakfast of broth and Jell-O.

"How are you this morning, Ms. Essie?" she said cheerfully

"I'm a little tired," Essie Mae said, hoping she wouldn't start a conversation. She really didn't feel like chatting.

"Oh, it's a beautiful day," the nurse said. "This is the day that the Lord has made. Let us rejoice and be glad in it!" she quoted the Bible Scripture and breezed on out the door with her cart of breakfast trays.

I wish I could rejoice, Essie Mae thought. I wonder who's going to take care of me. I do hate to be a burden, she told herself again. She thought of all of her family members, and not one of them was able to quit work to look after her. None of them were able to pay for a full-time nurse. *Oh, it would have been so much better if I had woke up in heaven,* she told herself. Just then, as if an angel whispered in her ear, she remembered Ms. Wilson's gift to her – "If you ever need anything, call Cynthia or Junior and they will take care of it for you." Essie Mae hated to call them, but she had no other choice.

By the time she was discharged from the hospital, a full-time nurse was at her door to greet her. She was pleasant and very gentle. Essie Mae liked her from the start. When she found out she was a Christian, she liked her even more. She later found out that one of the requirements for the job was that she had to be a Christian. Ms. Cynthia had thought of that so Essie Mae would have someone she could relate to and to pray with. They prayed and talked about the Bible every day.

That Christmas had come and went and another one was approaching. It had been almost a year since Essie Mae had that near fatal heart attack. But thanks to the good home care she was getting from the nurse the Wilson family hired, she was doing great. She could move about the house, sit on the porch which she and the nurse did a lot during the warm days of spring and early summer and early fall. She was even able to attend church now and then. She appeared to be doing so well that everyone stopped being concerned for her. But Essie Mae had this knowing in her spirit that she would be leaving this world soon. She didn't share this knowing with her family. She had mentioned it to Maggie, her nurse and now her friend, but she always took it as a joke and made fun and laughed. Essie Mae would laugh too. But she knew.

CHAPTER 12

In just three weeks, Nina would be taking her final exams after four long years. Another month or so, and she would graduate. She'd maintained an A/B average and she was happy. She thought of how proud her grandmother would be to see her march in her cap and gown with a degree in hand. Like all of her other grandchildren and great-grandchildren's graduations. Whether high school or college, Essie Mae was right there at each ceremony. She would be so proud and would let anyone who'd listen know it. Nina couldn't wait to see her great-grandmother beam with pride on her graduation day. She had three more tests to take with the hardest being her journalism class. The professor in that class gave hard exams. He told the class on the first day, *"If you pass this class, you are sure to become a great journalist. I do not give easy tests. When you leave this class, you will know your stuff."* So far, Nina had passed every one of his exams. She didn't want to fail the final one, so she planned to study most of the night.

Suddenly the door opened and her roommate rushed in.

"Girl, I just heard about this great party going on over at this fraternity house. Me and the girls are going. Why don't you come along, Nina?"

"No, thank you. I have a test to study for."

"You are always studying, girl. When are you going to have some fun?" Wanda said, flinging clothes here and there, looking for something to wear.

"I have fun. But when I have to study, I study," Nina said.

"What kind of fun do you have when the only time you go out is to a Bible study? How much fun can that be? You're too goody-goody. There have been a lot of good-looking guys asking about you. I can get you lots of dates if you would just loosen up," Wanda said.

"I can find my own dates, thank you," Nina said. "If you ask me, you're too loose. You need to slow down and get serious about your studies."

"Don't worry about me and my grades. People go to college to have fun, not just to study all the time. Are you coming with me to the party?"

"No."

"Ah, come on, Nina. It'll be fun."

"Will you come with me to Bible study next week?"

"No."

"Ah, come on, Wanda. It'll be fun," Nina said, using Wanda's words and tone.

Wanda saw that she wasn't getting anywhere with Nina and walked out of the door saying, "Don't wait up."

Nina thought Wanda was right that she was very selective of what type of entertainment she got involved in. The few dates she had gone on never led to anything serious. She was so straight that the guys found her to be little fun. When she was tempted to let her guard down, she would hear her Grandma Essie's voice, "Child don't you give your all to no man until you are ready to get married. They'll take everything and leave you holding the bag. Do you hear me, Child?" "Yes, Grandma," would be her reply. So she hung with the safe groups and clean fun. She didn't mind. She had goals, and she wasn't about to let having "fun" get in the way of them.

After Wanda left, Nina picked up her journalism book and began to study for her next exam. The ringing of the phone startled her awake. She had dozed off while reading. She looked at the clock and it said 12:00. She glanced over at Wanda's bed; it was empty.

"Hello," Nina said, yawning.

"Nina, honey," her mother said in a tone that made Nina react in alarm.

"What's wrong, Mom?" she asked. Her heart began to pound. Had something happened to her Dad or her brother, she wondered"

"It's Grandma."

"No. What happened?" she almost screamed.

"She's had another heart attack. It's serious. She's

talking about going home. I think you better come home. She's asking for you."

"Do you think Daddy can come and get me?" Nina asked. "He'll be there in the morning," her mother told her.

After she hung up the phone, Nina knew she couldn't concentrate any further on her studies, so she went to bed and thought of the many wonderful moments she had spent with her great-grandmother. Now she may be dying. "Dear Lord," she prayed, "please don't take her before I get there."

The morning dawned as dreary as she felt. Her dad would pick her up at ten. She tried to pack but couldn't decide what to put into her suitcase. She picked up and put down the same sweater three times. Now and then she'd let out a long sigh as she walked the small space of her dorm room. At ten she heard a knock on the door. Her suitcase was packed, but she couldn't remember what she had in it. She walked to the car without saying much more that hello to her dad. His face was very solemn.

After two hours of riding, they pulled into the driveway of the house Nina had spent many happy hours visiting her special great-grandmother. She felt a renewed sadness rise up in her. Inside, her mother sat by the bed holding Essie Mae's hand. Nina stood by the door and watched a moment. Then she rushed forward and laid her head on Essie Mae's chest.

"Oh, Grandma, Grandma," she said through tears.

"Nina, Baby. Nina, Child. Don't cry. I'm glad you're

here. I didn't want to go without saying good-bye. I can go in peace now," she whispered. "Promise me you'll write that book. Tell the whole story, you hear?"

"I promise, Grandma," Nina said through tears. "I love you, Grandma. I'm going to miss you so much."

"I love you too, Baby," Essie Mae said, speaking barely above a whisper. It was such a strain for her to talk. Then she said with much more strength, "She's here, Nina!"

"Who's here, Grandma?" Nina asked.

"My angel. Don't you see her over there?"

Nina looked around the room but didn't see anyone but her parents and Maggie, the nurse. When she looked back at her grandmother, she could see her lips moving but couldn't hear any words. Shortly after that Nina heard her gasp and her chest rose and fell and then she was still. Nina burst into tears and her mother and father led her out of the room while Maggie checked for a heartbeat. Finding none, she called the doctor. Essie Mae was gone at the age of eighty-nine. This time when she woke up, she would not be disappointed, she would awake to the singing of the heavenly angels.

Nina tried to be strong at the funeral. But the tears wouldn't stop flowing. Oh, how she would miss her great-grandma. She would greatly miss looking out into the audience and seeing the proud look on her face at her graduation. She would miss her prayers, her cooking, the great advice she so wisely gave. But mostly, she would miss the summer visits on the porch.

The church was overflowing. Even some of the

Wilsons' grandchildren were there. She had invited Essie Mae's favorite quartet to sing. When they sang her favorite song, the whole church was on its feet clapping and singing along and remembering how Essie Mae used to walk the floor, slinging her handkerchief when those men sang that song. Oh, they had never sung it quite so well as they were doing then. What a memorable going away service, just like Essie Mae wanted. She always said, "I don't want no sad funeral, 'cause I ain't going to be sad. I'm going to be with Jesus."

At the gravesite, people gathered around to hear the pastor's last words *"ashes to ashes and dust to dust ..."* Nina scanned the crowd. She caught the eye of a very tall woman, dressed very neatly in a gray suit with her hair beautifully styled. Something about her made Nina feel a connection somehow, but she could not recall ever seeing her before. She leaned over and asked her mother who was the very tall lady. When they looked, she was gone. She saw her once more in the fellowship hall after the funeral. She wasn't eating. She was standing by the door. Nina tried to reach her, but people kept stopping her, offering condolences. She tried to be kind and attentive to them, yet keep an eye on the woman. She glanced briefly at the person speaking to her. In that brief moment, the woman disappeared. Nina ran outside to see if she could catch her, but she was gone.

That night as she lay in bed going over the events of the funeral, feeling very sad, the face of the very tall lady came to her mind. She remembered when their eyes met, there seemed to be a message within the stare. Who was she and why hadn't anyone else noticed her? As Nina pondered all these things over in her mind, she suddenly sat straight up in bed. "Oh my God!" she said aloud. "Oh my God!" she repeated. "She's Grandma's angel! It must be. She looked just like Grandma described her-tall, immaculately dressed, and hair neat with every strand in place. It was her! No one else could see her. Only I could see her because Grandma wanted me to see her. Oh, Grandma, thank you. You didn't leave me alone, did you? She's my angel now, isn't she?" With that knowing, Nina fell asleep with a resolve that all was well with Grandma and all was well with her, too.

CHAPTER 13

Two years after graduation, Nina drove down the familiar street. On the seat beside her was the book. She had finished the book she'd promised to write. She was excited about it. The publisher thought she had done a great job telling the story of how God turned a wild, worldly woman into a mild, loving, godly woman who touched many lives. Nina wanted to share the finished product with her great- grandma the way she used to do when something exciting happened to her. She thought of going to the cemetery and chatting with her there. But no, she had to go to the place where she first heard the story. She turned into the driveway. She had no idea who lived there now, but the house looked the same. The swing and the chairs were still on the porch. Nina walked up the steps and took a seat in the chair her great-grandma used to sit in. It was summer and the memories of that hot, humid day nearly ten years before when they had to sit out on the porch because the air conditioner was broken, which made it too uncomfortable to stay inside, flooded her mind. That day Nina had looked at the scars on her great grandma's arms and asked, *"Grandma, how did you get those scars?"* A simple question like that took them on a journey of shock, sorrow, and joy. The finished book in her hand brought her to the end of that journey. "Here it is, Grandma," Nina said softly, as if she was there next to her. " Here's the book I promised to write. I told it all just like you told me. I think you would be proud of me. I love you, Grandma . I still miss you." She yearned to feel those loving arms around her. No one could hug like Grandma Essie, Nina thought.

No one came out while Nina sat visiting with her great-grandmother. After a while, she left the porch. She glanced back at the house and porch and knew this visit was the final step of her journey with her great-grandmother Essie Mae. Clutching the promised book in her hand, it was like saying "the end" as she got into her car and backed out of the driveway. Now she could start her own journey-making memories to share with her own children, grandchildren or even great-grandchildren – if God so allowed.